Generations

A Tradition of Timeless Recipes
The Junior League of Rockford

JUNIOR
LEAGUE
OF
ROCKFORD
INC.

This cookbook is a collection of favorite recipes, which are not necessarily original recipes.

Published by Junior League of Rockford, Inc.

Library of Congress Catalog Number: 94-71858
ISBN: 0-87197-408-8

Manufactured by
Favorite Recipes© Press
P.O. Box 305142
Nashville, Tennessee 37230
1-800-358-0560

Manufactured in the United States of America
First Printing: 1994   15,000 copies

enerations is thankfully dedicated to the active, sustaining, and provisional members of the Junior League of Rockford, their families and friends, and the community members who came together and created a classic.

Contents

Recipes are like poems; they keep what kept us.
Henri Coulette

*It's Food too fine for angels; yet come, take and eat
thy fill! It's Heaven's sugar cake.*   Author Unknown

*To make a good soup, the pot must only simmer,
or "smile."*   French Proverb

Eternity is two people and a roast turkey.   James Dent
Wine is sunlight, held together by water.   Galileo

*What is Patriotism but the love of good things we
ate in our childhood.*   Lin Yutang

*What was paradise, but a garden full of
vegetables and herbs and pleasure. Nothing
there but delights.*   William Lawson

Foreword

"The true cook holds in his palm the happiness of mankind, the welfare of GENERATIONS yet unborn."
—*Norman Douglas*

Generation to generation we capture our history through three essentials—film, food, and feelings.

Sepia, black and white, or color—our photographs allow us to remember those who have passed before and with us. How wonderful to be able to recall our grandparents' wedding celebration, a favorite uncle's birthday party, or a special couples' anniversary dinner.

These portraits are our windows into each generation's life, whether we were there or not!

Just as these snapshots are handed down, so, too, are our culinary traditions. Both preserve our family's heritage. Though the family grows and changes, food is a constant.

Travel the world and we encounter new preparations, new ingredients, new forms of these foods. Still, we long for the hearth and home that has created us.

A family—no matter how large, no matter how small—together means home and encompasses the traditions of generations. Birthday parties, Fourth of July picnics, Thanksgiving dinners, each includes its special dishes in order to be complete.

The German chocolate cake that is Dad's favorite, Aunt Mae's delicious baked beans, the turkey dressing only Grandma Carriar could create—all harken back to memorable times spent with special people. And, although they may be gone, their spirits survive through the comforts derived from the food we eat because of them.

We draw comfort from knowing that our past, a part of our present, will always be an integral piece of our future. For as each generation adds its photos and recipes to the collection, new traditions are created. They allow us to feel the sentiments felt by GENERATIONS before us.

OPEN-FACED BRIE APPETIZERS

Serves 6 to 8

A California Cabernet Sauvignon is great with these appetizers.

1   loaf French bread
    Olive oil
8   ounces mushrooms, thickly sliced
1/2 medium red onion, coarsely chopped
1/2 red bell pepper, coarsely chopped
1/2 yellow bell pepper, coarsely chopped
2   tablespoons butter
1/2 teaspoon thyme
    Freshly ground pepper to taste
5   ounces Brie cheese, sliced

Cut the French bread into 1/2-inch slices. Brush with olive oil; place on a baking sheet. Toast until light brown.

Sauté the mushrooms, onion and bell peppers in butter in a sauté pan until tender. Stir in the thyme and pepper. Spoon onto toast on baking sheet; top with a slice of cheese. Broil just until the cheese melts. Serve immediately.

BRIOLOTTA

Serves 12 to 16

These sausage-stuffed pastries are outstanding appetizers for all special occasions.

1   package frozen puff pastry
1   pound Italian sausage
8   ounces mushrooms, sliced
1   can artichoke hearts, drained, chopped
2   cups shredded Swiss cheese
1   egg, beaten
1   tablespoon water

Thaw the puff pastry sheets for 30 minutes. Brown the sausage in a skillet, stirring until crumbly; drain well. Roll the pastry sheets to 12x18-inch rectangles on a floured surface. Sprinkle each rectangle with half the sausage, mushrooms, artichokes and cheese. Roll up the pastry from the wide side to enclose filling; press the ends and edges to seal. Place on a baking sheet. Brush with a mixture of egg and water. Bake at 375 degrees for 20 to 25 minutes or until golden brown. Serve immediately.

Acknowledgements

Junior League of Rockford, Inc.
Cookbook Committee Members

Co-Chairmen
  Barbara Carlson Mueller
  Sharon Nelson

Vice Chairman
  Maureen Basile

Business Manager
  Debra Cyborski

Marketing Director
  Christyn Divine

Marketing Vice Directors
  Marianne Marshall
  Suzanne Floody

Art Director
  Patricia Shepherd

Special Events
  Jane Nappi-Lindstrand

Sales/Distribution
  Mary Ann Fearer

Testing Chairmen
  Barbara Kaiser
  Patricia Harker

Sustaining Members
  Mary-Stuart Carruthers
  Ellen Letourneau
  Suzanne Sloan
  Judy Larson

Special Acknowledgements:

Photography
  Stephen Pitkin

Stylist
  Karen Nielsen

Color Separations and Film Assembly
  Professional Graphics

Graphic Design Consultants
  Design Graphics

Wine Recommendations
  Joe Valaitis

APPETIZERS & BEVERAGES

It's Food too fine for angels; yet come,
take and eat thy fill! It's Heaven's sugar cake.

Author Unknown

OPEN-FACED BRIE APPETIZERS

Serves 6 to 8

A California Cabernet Sauvignon is great with these appetizers.

1   loaf French bread
      Olive oil
8   ounces mushrooms, thickly sliced
1/2   medium red onion, coarsely chopped
1/2   red bell pepper, coarsely chopped
1/2   yellow bell pepper, coarsely chopped
2   tablespoons butter
1/2   teaspoon thyme
      Freshly ground pepper to taste
5   ounces Brie cheese, sliced

Cut the French bread into 1/2-inch slices. Brush with olive oil; place on a baking sheet. Toast until light brown.

Sauté the mushrooms, onion and bell peppers in butter in a sauté pan until tender. Stir in the thyme and pepper. Spoon onto toast on baking sheet; top with a slice of cheese. Broil just until the cheese melts. Serve immediately.

BRIOLOTTA

Serves 12 to 16

These sausage-stuffed pastries are outstanding appetizers for all special occasions.

1   package frozen puff pastry
1   pound Italian sausage
8   ounces mushrooms, sliced
1   can artichoke hearts, drained, chopped
2   cups shredded Swiss cheese
1   egg, beaten
1   tablespoon water

Thaw the puff pastry sheets for 30 minutes. Brown the sausage in a skillet, stirring until crumbly; drain well. Roll the pastry sheets to 12x18-inch rectangles on a floured surface. Sprinkle each rectangle with half the sausage, mushrooms, artichokes and cheese. Roll up the pastry from the wide side to enclose filling; press the ends and edges to seal. Place on a baking sheet. Brush with a mixture of egg and water. Bake at 375 degrees for 20 to 25 minutes or until golden brown. Serve immediately.

Kent Lindstrand, 2½, and his sister,
Karen, 6½, watch as their mother, Mrs. Doe
Lindstrand, prepares fruit punch, using ice
cream as a base. The Lindstrands live at
1425 Green st.

Housewife from Germany
Likes Ice Cream Punch

APPETIZERS & BEVERAGES

It's Food too fine for angels; yet come,
take and eat thy fill! It's Heaven's sugar cake.

Author Unknown

$\mathscr{A}$cknowledgements

Junior League of Rockford, Inc.
Cookbook Committee Members

Co-Chairmen
Barbara Carlson Mueller
Sharon Nelson

Vice Chairman
Maureen Basile

Business Manager
Debra Cyborski

Marketing Director
Christyn Divine

Marketing Vice Directors
Marianne Marshall
Suzanne Floody

Art Director
Patricia Shepherd

Special Events
Jane Nappi-Lindstrand

Sales/Distribution
Mary Ann Fearer

Testing Chairmen
Barbara Kaiser
Patricia Harker

Sustaining Members
Mary-Stuart Carruthers
Ellen Letourneau
Suzanne Sloan
Judy Larson

Special Acknowledgements:

Photography
Stephen Pitkin

Stylist
Karen Nielsen

Color Separations and Film Assembly
Professional Graphics

Graphic Design Consultants
Design Graphics

Wine Recommendations
Joe Valaitis

PESTO BRIE

Serves 8

A very colorful, quick and easy appetizer.

1	pound Brie cheese
1	plum tomato, seeded, chopped
2	green onions, thinly sliced
1/4	cup pesto
1	loaf French bread, sliced, toasted

Trim the rind from the cheese and cut the cheese into chunks. Layer the cheese, tomato and green onions in a baking dish. Dot with the pesto. Bake at 350 degrees until the cheese melts and the pesto begins to run. Serve warm with bread slices.

CHEDDAR CHEESE TARTS

Serves 16

This is an American adaptation of an authentic French cheese tart. It is possible to reduce the crème fraîche and butter and add some good dark beer to maintain the moisture in the recipe.

The dough

1/2	cup lukewarm milk
1	envelope dry yeast
2	(to 2 1/4) cups unbleached flour
2	large eggs
1/2	teaspoon salt
6	tablespoons butter

The tarts

16	ounces extra-sharp Cheddar cheese, thinly sliced
2	large eggs
2	large egg yolks
1	cup Crème Fraîche (page 194) or sour cream
1/4	cup unsalted butter
	Freshly grated nutmeg to taste
	Salt and freshly ground pepper to taste

Combine the milk, yeast and 1/4 cup of the flour in a large mixer bowl; mix until smooth. Let stand for 5 minutes. Stir in the remaining flour, eggs and salt. Add the butter gradually, working in with fingers to form dough. Knead on a floured surface for 5 minutes or until smooth and elastic, kneading in additional flour if needed to form a soft and slightly sticky dough. Place in a large greased bowl, turning to coat surface. Let rise for 1 1/2 hours or until doubled in bulk. Punch the dough down and divide into 2 portions. Press each portion over the bottom of a buttered 10-inch ceramic baking dish.

Arrange the cheese evenly over the dough. Whisk the eggs, egg yolks and Crème Fraîche in a bowl until smooth. Spread over the cheese. Dot with butter; sprinkle with nutmeg, salt and pepper. Bake at 375 degrees for 35 minutes or until brown and bubbly.

HONEY CURRY DIP

Serves 8 to 10

Serve this dip with fresh or blanched vegetables or pita bread for dipping.

2   cups mayonnaise
3   tablespoons catsup
3   tablespoons honey
3   tablespoons chopped onion
1   teaspoon lemon juice
1   tablespoon curry powder
1   teaspoon cayenne pepper

Combine the mayonnaise, catsup, honey, onion, lemon juice, curry powder and cayenne pepper in a bowl; mix well. Chill, covered, for 8 hours or longer.

PEPPERONI PIZZA DIP

Serves 12

Crackers or bagel chips are good with this dip.

8   ounces cream cheese, softened
1/2   cup sour cream
1   teaspoon oregano, crushed
1/2   teaspoon garlic powder
1/8   teaspoon crushed red pepper
1/2   cup pizza sauce
1/2   cup chopped pepperoni
1/4   cup chopped green onions
1/4   cup chopped green bell pepper
1/2   cup shredded mozzarella cheese

Combine the cream cheese, sour cream, oregano, garlic powder and red pepper in a bowl; mix well. Spread in a shallow 9-inch or 10-inch baking dish. Spread the pizza sauce over the top. Sprinkle with the pepperoni, green onions and green pepper. Bake at 350 degrees for 10 minutes. Sprinkle with cheese. Bake for 5 minutes longer or until the cheese melts.

EGGPLANT CAVIAR

Serves 10 to 12

A great way to serve eggplant! Serve chilled with thinly sliced pumpernickel or rye bread.

1	large eggplant
1	large onion, chopped
1	green bell pepper, chopped
1	clove of garlic, minced
1/2	cup olive oil
2	tomatoes, peeled, chopped
	Salt and pepper to taste
2	tablespoons dry white wine

Bake the whole eggplant at 400 degrees for 1 hour or until tender. Peel and chop fine.

Sauté the onion, green pepper and garlic in olive oil in a skillet until tender but not brown. Add the eggplant, tomatoes, salt and pepper; mix well. Stir in the wine. Cook until thickened. Spoon into a serving bowl. Chill until serving time.

GARDEN FRESH SALSA

Serves 12

A very colorful, easy and refreshing salsa. Add a can of chopped green chilies for extra zip.

2	(16-ounce) cans whole peeled tomatoes
2	medium jalapeño peppers, chopped
1	small red chili pepper
4	green onions, chopped
1/2	bunch cilantro, chopped
	Juice of 1 lime
1	teaspoon garlic powder
	Salt and pepper to taste

Drain and chop the tomatoes. Combine with the peppers, green onions, cilantro, lime juice, garlic powder, salt and pepper in a bowl; mix well. Chill until serving time. Store in the refrigerator for up to 2 weeks.

FRESH CORN TORTILLA CHIPS

Serves 6 to 8

Every cookbook should have this recipe for tortilla chips; they are much better than commercial chips. Serve them with fresh salsa or guacamole.

2	packages corn tortillas
2	(to 4) cups vegetable oil
	Salt to taste

Stack 3 or 4 tortillas together and cut into 8 equal wedges. Heat the oil in a large skillet over medium heat. Add the tortilla wedges in a single layer. Fry for 1 to 2 minutes; turn chips. Fry until light brown; drain. May salt the chips lightly if desired.

SHANGHAI EGG ROLLS

Serves 15 to 20

A different appetizer with an Asian flavor!

1   pound ground beef
1   small carrot, finely chopped
1   onion, finely chopped
2   teaspoons peanut butter
    Soy sauce to taste
    Salt and pepper to taste
15   (to 20) egg roll or won ton wrappers
    Peanut oil for deep frying

Brown the ground beef with the carrot and onion in a skillet, stirring frequently; drain. Add the peanut butter, soy sauce, salt and pepper; mix well. Spoon the mixture onto the egg roll wrappers. Seal the edges with a paste of flour and water. Deep-fry in hot peanut oil until golden brown. Drain and serve immediately.

GOAT CHEESE AND PISTACHIO SPREAD

Serves 8

Garnish this with chive blades. It can be made up to 2 days in advance and chilled until serving time.

1   large clove of garlic
1   teaspoon salt
3   (3½-inch) rolls Montrachet or other goat cheese
½   cup unsalted butter, softened
¼   cup toasted chopped pistachios
¼   cup chopped chives
    Salt and pepper to taste
1   loaf French bread, sliced ¼ inch thick, toasted

Crush the garlic to a paste with the 1 teaspoon salt in a bowl. Add the cheese, butter, pistachios, chopped chives, salt and pepper. Beat until smooth. Spread in a serving dish. Chill, covered with plastic wrap, until serving time. Serve with the toasted French bread.

MEXICAN FUDGE

Serves 36

This very quick and easy appetizer may also be served warm as a breakfast dish.

3   eggs
1/2   cup green taco sauce
8   ounces Cheddar cheese, shredded
8   ounces Monterey Jack cheese, shredded

Beat the eggs in a bowl. Add the taco sauce; mix well. Sprinkle half the cheeses in a greased 9x9-inch baking pan. Spread the egg mixture over the cheese; sprinkle with the remaining cheese. Bake at 350 degrees for 30 minutes. Cool. Cut into small squares.

SUN-DRIED TOMATO-STUFFED MUSHROOMS

Serves 8

The intense flavor of sun-dried tomatoes, long a favorite in Italy, enhances this favorite appetizer.

12   ounces oil-pack sun-dried tomatoes
24   mushrooms
1/3   cup finely chopped shallots
1   teaspoon chopped garlic
1/8   teaspoon thyme
      Salt and pepper to taste
3   tablespoons whipping cream
      Freshly grated Parmesan cheese

Drain the tomatoes, reserving 1/4 cup of the oil; mince the tomatoes. Remove the mushroom stems and chop the stems to measure 1 cup. Brush the mushroom caps lightly with some of the reserved oil; arrange round side up on a rack in a broiler pan. Broil 6 inches from the heat source for 2 minutes or until they begin to soften. Arrange the mushrooms round side down on a baking sheet.

Sauté the shallots and garlic in the remaining reserved oil in a large skillet until tender. Stir in the mushroom stems, tomatoes, thyme, salt and pepper. Cook for 6 minutes or until the liquid has evaporated. Stir in the cream.

Spoon the mixture into the mushroom caps; sprinkle with the Parmesan cheese. Bake at 350 degrees for 12 minutes.

MARINATED MUSHROOMS

Serves 10 to 12

Serve these with wooden picks as an appetizer or on a bed of lettuce as a salad, using the marinade as the dressing.

1   pound fresh mushrooms
1/2 cup wine vinegar
1/2 cup vegetable oil
1   clove of garlic, minced
1   tablespoon thinly sliced chives or green onion tops
1   bay leaf
1   teaspoon salt

Clean the mushrooms, trimming the bottom of the stems. Combine the vinegar, oil, garlic, chives, bay leaf and salt in a bowl; mix well. Add the mushrooms. Marinate in the refrigerator for 4 hours to overnight. Discard the bay leaf. Serve at room temperature; do not drain.

ONION PARMESAN PUFFS

Serves 24

These are delicious and easy to make, although they look as if they require a lot of work. They are especially good with hearty winter soups.

2   cups chopped onions
1/4 cup unsalted butter
1 1/2 cups water
1/2 cup unsalted butter
1 1/2 cups flour
6   eggs, at room temperature
2   teaspoons salt
1 1/2 cups freshly grated Parmesan cheese
     Several tablespoons milk
     Additional Parmesan cheese

Sauté the onions in 1/4 cup butter in a skillet until tender; set aside.

Bring the water to a boil in a saucepan. Stir in 1/2 cup butter until melted. Add the flour all at once; mixing well. Cook until the mixture forms a ball and pulls from the side of the pan; remove from the heat. Beat in the eggs 1 at a time. Add salt, 1 1/2 cups cheese and sautéed onions; mix well.

Drop the mixture by heaping tablespoonfuls onto a greased baking sheet. Brush the tops with milk; sprinkle with the cheese. Bake at 400 degrees for 35 to 40 minutes or until golden brown.

PATE BEAU MONDE

Serves 8

The wonderful and unique flavor of this dip is good with your favorite fresh vegetables.

8 ounces cream cheese, softened
2¹/2 teaspoons Beau Monde seasoning
¹/4 teaspoon thyme
¹/4 teaspoon marjoram
¹/4 teaspoon savory
1 teaspoon chopped parsley

Mix the cream cheese, Beau Monde seasoning, thyme, marjoram, savory and parsley in a bowl. Chill for several hours to overnight. Serve at room temperature.

PUREE OF RED PEPPER

Serves 8 to 10

This recipe provides the basic purée for the following three recipes. It can be stored in the refrigerator for up to two weeks or frozen for up to six months and is a good way to use red peppers from the garden at the end of the summer.

8 pounds large red bell peppers
²/3 cup olive oil
1 teaspoon thyme
1¹/2 teaspoons salt
¹/4 teaspoon cayenne pepper

Slice the peppers into ¹/2-inch strips, discarding the stems and seeds. Heat the olive oil in a large skillet. Add the peppers, thyme, salt and cayenne pepper. Simmer, covered, for 30 minutes, stirring occasionally. Spoon into a colander; drain for 10 minutes. Process in a food processor in 3 batches until smooth. Press the mixture through a fine sieve to remove any remaining skin. Drain in a fine sieve for 30 minutes to remove excess liquid. Use in the following recipes or store in the refrigerator or freezer.

RED PEPPER MOUSSELINES

Serves 8

The color adds so much to your menu. Serve mousselines in their molds or unmold onto serving plates. Garnish them with Crème Fraîche (page 194), black caviar and parsley.

4 large eggs
1 cup whipping cream
2 cups Purée of Red Pepper (recipe above)
¹/2 teaspoon salt

Beat the eggs in a bowl. Add the cream, Purée of Red Pepper and salt; mix gently for 20 to 30 seconds or until smooth. Spoon into 8 buttered ¹/2-cup ovenproof molds. Place in a pan with enough hot water to reach ²/3 of the way up sides. Bake at 400 degrees for 40 to 45 minutes or until a tester inserted in the center of a mold comes out clean. Loosen the mousselines with a knife to remove.

RED PEPPER CAVIAR

Serves 8 to 10

Serve this colorful mixture with fresh or steamed vegetables such as broccoli, cauliflower, summer squash or zucchini.

2   cups Purée of Red Pepper (page 19)
2   large egg yolks
1/2   cup olive oil
1/2   teaspoon salt
      Freshly ground black pepper or cayenne pepper to taste

Combine the Purée of Red Pepper and egg yolks in a food processor container fitted with a metal blade. Process for 15 seconds or until smooth. Add the olive oil gradually, processing constantly until smooth. Season with salt and pepper. Chill, covered, for up to 1 week.

RED PEPPER TOASTS

Serves 12

These are good as an appetizer or as an accompaniment for soups. You can make as many toasts as you need.

12   slices French bread
      Butter or garlic-flavored olive oil
      Purée of Red Pepper (page 19)
      Grated Gruyère cheese or other cheese

Spread the bread slices with butter; place on a baking sheet. Toast until light brown. Spread with the Purée of Red Pepper; sprinkle with cheese. Bake at 400 degrees until light brown.

SALMON MOUSSE

Serves 8 to 10

This is especially pretty made in a fish mold, spread with a thin layer of mayonnaise and garnished with pimento, cucumber slices and parsley.

4   eggs
1/2   small jar pimento
1   can peas, drained
1   cup milk
1/4   teaspoon nutmeg
1/4   teaspoon each salt and pepper
1   (14-ounce) can salmon, drained

Combine the eggs, pimento, peas, milk, nutmeg, salt and pepper in a blender container; process for 30 seconds. Flake the salmon, discarding the skin and bones. Add to the blender container. Process just until salmon is mixed. Spoon into a greased mold; place in a large pan with 1 inch of boiling water. Bake at 425 degrees for 40 minutes. Cool to room temperature. Chill until set. Unmold onto a serving platter and garnish.

SAUSAGE STARS

Serves 48

Men like these appetizers. Chopped onions, mushrooms and green peppers can also be added.

1   **pound pork or Italian sausage**
1½   **cups shredded sharp Cheddar cheese**
1½   **cups shredded Monterey Jack cheese**
1   **cup sliced black olives**
½   **cup chopped red bell pepper**
1   **cup ranch salad dressing**
1   **package won ton wrappers**
      Vegetable oil

Cook the sausage in a skillet, stirring until crumbly; drain. Combine the sausage with the cheeses, olives, bell pepper and salad dressing in a bowl; mix well.

Brush the won ton wrappers with oil and press 1 wrapper into each of 48 lightly greased 2-inch muffin cups. Bake at 350 degrees for 5 to 8 minutes or until golden brown. Remove to a baking sheet. Fill with the sausage mixture. Bake for 5 minutes or until bubbly.

BLACKENED SHRIMP

Serves 2 to 4

This is a classic shrimp recipe with the unpeeled shrimp served with French bread, lots of napkins and bowls for the shells. For a cocktail party, the shrimp can be prepared peeled without loss of flavor.

1   **pound unpeeled large shrimp**
½   **cup unsalted butter**
1½   **teaspoons minced garlic**
1   **teaspoon Worcestershire sauce**
4   **(to 5) teaspoons Seafood Magic**
5   **tablespoons unsalted butter**
½   **cup bottled clam juice**
¼   **cup beer, at room temperature**

Rinse and drain the shrimp. Combine ½ cup butter, garlic, Worcestershire sauce and Seafood Magic in a large skillet over high heat. Heat until the butter melts. Add the shrimp. Cook for 2 minutes, shaking pan back and forth constantly; do not stir. Add 5 tablespoons butter and clam juice. Cook for 2 minutes, shaking pan. Add beer. Cook for 1 minute, shaking pan.

KEY WEST SHRIMP

Serves 4 to 6

You may also use peeled cooked shrimp in this recipe and bake at 400 degrees for 10 minutes.

2   pounds unpeeled jumbo shrimp
2   limes
1   orange
1/2 cup butter, sliced
1   (16-ounce) bottle of zesty Italian salad dressing
1/4 cup white wine
1/2 teaspoon chopped fresh basil
1   teaspoon cracked peppercorns

Place the unpeeled shrimp in a baking dish. Squeeze the juice from the limes and orange over the shrimp; place the squeezed limes and orange in the baking dish with shrimp. Dot with butter. Pour a mixture of the salad dressing, wine, basil and peppercorns over the top. Bake at 500 degrees for 15 minutes; do not overcook. Serve with French bread.

TOMATO PHYLLO PIZZA

Serves 8 to 10

Save this recipe to try with vine-ripened summer tomatoes rather than with the out-of-season varieties that bear little resemblance to their juicy, flavorful ideal.

7   sheets phyllo dough
5   tablespoons melted unsalted butter
7   tablespoons freshly grated Parmesan cheese
1   cup shredded mozzarella cheese
1   cup thinly sliced purple onion
2   pounds vine-ripened tomatoes
1/2 teaspoon oregano
1   teaspoon fresh thyme or 1/4 teaspoon dried thyme
     Salt and pepper to taste

Layer the phyllo dough on a large buttered baking sheet, brushing each sheet lightly with butter and sprinkling all but the last sheet with 1 tablespoon Parmesan cheese. Press the layers together. Top with the mozzarella cheese and onion. Slice the tomatoes 1/4 inch thick. Arrange in a single layer over the top. Sprinkle with the remaining 1 tablespoon Parmesan cheese, oregano, thyme, salt and pepper. Bake on the center oven rack at 375 degrees for 30 to 35 minutes or until golden brown. Cut into squares to serve; garnish with fresh basil or oregano.

CONFETTI VEGETABLE TERRINE

Serves 12

Press parsley onto the sides of this terrine and garnish the top with edible flowers, using chives for the stems. Serve it with crackers.

16   ounces cream cheese, softened
1/2 cup crumbled feta cheese
1/4 teaspoon garlic powder
1/8 teaspoon ground red pepper
1/2 cup sour cream
2   eggs
1 1/2 teaspoons finely grated lemon rind
1/4 cup thinly sliced green onions
1/2 cup chopped pimentos
1/3 cup chopped black olives

Line the bottom of a 4x8-inch loaf pan with foil; grease the sides. Beat the cream cheese in a medium mixer bowl until smooth. Add feta cheese, garlic powder and red pepper; mix well. Add sour cream, eggs and lemon rind; beat just until blended. Stir in green onions, pimentos and olives. Spread evenly in prepared pan. Place in a larger baking pan with 1 inch of boiling water. Bake at 325 degrees for 50 minutes or until the center is soft set. Cool completely in the pan on a wire rack. Chill, covered, for 4 to 24 hours. Loosen the edges of the terrine with a knife; invert onto a serving plate lined with fresh purple kale or leaf lettuce, discarding foil. Garnish as desired.

BLACK RASPBERRY MELBA PUNCH

Serves 16

This festive punch is great for holiday entertaining. It is made with Chambord, a dessert liqueur that combines the flavors of small black raspberries with honey and herbs.

1   cup Chambord
1   (6-ounce) can frozen lemonade concentrate, partially thawed
1/2 cup Rose's lime juice
1/2 cup fresh lemon juice
1   quart sparkling water
1   bottle of Champagne

Combine the Chambord, lemonade concentrate, lime juice and lemon juice in a punch bowl; mix well. Add the sparkling water and Champagne, mixing gently. Add an ice ring. Serve in punch cups.

PRANCER'S PUNCH

Serves 6 to 8

The beautiful red color of this punch makes it perfect for Christmas entertaining.

1   (12-ounce) package frozen pitted dark sweet cherries, thawed
1   (1-liter) bottle of cider, chilled
2   cups cranberry juice cocktail, chilled
1¹/₂ cups seltzer water, chilled
3   tablespoons fresh lime juice
1   lime

Combine the cherries, cider, cranberry juice, seltzer water and lime juice in a punch bowl or 2-quart pitcher; mix well. Cut the lime into halves lengthwise; slice crosswise into thin slices. Add to the punch. Serve in punch cups.

PREGNANT CANARY

Serves 1

A refreshing summer drink—an Orange Julius with a different spin.

3   ounces orange juice
2   ounces Triple Sec
2   ounces whipping cream

Combine the orange juice, Triple Sec and cream with crushed ice in a blender container; process until smooth.

THE RECIPE

Serves 6

This light and refreshing drink also may be made without the rum.

9   cups water
1   cup sugar
1   (12-ounce) can frozen lemonade concentrate
1   (12-ounce) can frozen orange juice concentrate
2   cups rum
    7-Up to fill glasses

Combine the water and sugar in a saucepan. Boil for 5 minutes. Add the lemonade concentrate, orange juice concentrate and rum; mix well. Simmer for 5 to 10 minutes. Pour into plastic freezer containers. Freeze, covered, for 24 hours. Spoon into glasses. Fill glasses with 7-Up; mix gently.

TRINIDAD TEMPTER

Serves 4

Serve this over ice for a refreshing drink. It is also good without the rum.

1³/4 cups orange juice
1¹/2 cups pineapple juice
2 tablespoons fresh lemon juice
¹/2 cup grenadine
1 teaspoons bitters
1 egg white
6 ounces rum

Combine the orange juice, pineapple juice, lemon juice, grenadine, bitters, egg white and rum in blender container; process for several seconds or until frothy.

HOT BUTTERED RUM MIX

Serves 50 to 80

This makes enough for a party or to keep in the freezer all winter for those cold evenings by the fire. Top the servings with whipped cream and nutmeg.

2 cups butter, softened
2 cups sugar
2 cups packed light brown sugar
3 tablespoons cinnamon
¹/4 teaspoon nutmeg
4 teaspoons rum extract
¹/2 gallon vanilla ice cream

Cream the butter, sugar and brown sugar in a mixer bowl until light and fluffy. Add the cinnamon, nutmeg and rum extract; mix well. Beat in the ice cream. Spoon into a freezer container. Combine 2 to 3 tablespoons of the mix with 1 jigger of rum in a mug for each serving. Fill the mug with boiling water, stirring to blend well.

Soups & Salads

Apple Soup with Roquefort Croutons, 29

Cold Raspberry Soup, 30

Avgolemono, 30

Bean Blanco Especial, 31

Black Bean Chili, 31

Bookbinder Soup, 32

Chicken and Crab Gumbo, 32

Chicken and Sausage Gumbo, 33

Curried Butternut Squash Soup, 34

Elegant Mushroom Soup, 34

Minestrone, 35

Onion Soup, 36

Potage a la Florentine, 36

Potato Soup, 37

Taffy Apple Salad, 37

Bing Cherry Salad, 38

Peach Salad, 38

Greek-Style Beef Salad, 39

Chicken Rice Salad with Artichokes, 39

Chicken and Grape Salad, 40

Asian Chicken Salad, 40

Asian Chicken Slaw, 41

Honey and Lime Chicken Salad, 41

Summertime Sea Shell Salad, 42

Chicken Waldorf, 42

Won Ton Chicken Salad, 43

Marinated Salmon Salad, 43

Smoked Salmon Caesar Salad, 44

Charbroiled Shrimp Caesar Salad, 45

Bow Tie Spinach Salad, 45

Caesar Pasta Primavera, 46

Picnic Pasta Salad, 46

Walnut and Avocado Salad, 47

Mexican Bean Salad, 47

Broccoli Salad, 48

Oriental Coleslaw, 48

Greek Salad, 49

Bleu Cheese Salad, 50

Sesame Spinach Salad, 50

German Potato Salad, 51

Sauerkraut Salad, 51

APPLE SOUP WITH ROQUEFORT CROUTONS

Serves 6

This hearty yet elegant soup is the perfect starter on a chilly evening. It tastes even better when reheated the second day.

The croutons

18	(1/4-inch) slices French bread
4	ounces Roquefort cheese, crumbled
1/4	cup unsalted butter, softened

The soup

1 1/4	pounds red Delicious apples, peeled, sliced
1 1/4	pounds Granny Smith apples, peeled, sliced
1	cup chopped onion
1	teaspoon minced garlic
1/4	cup melted unsalted butter
5	cups chicken stock
1 1/2	cups whipping cream
1/4	cup Calvados
	Salt and freshly ground pepper to taste
1/2	red Delicious apple
1/2	Granny Smith apple
1	tablespoon fresh lemon juice
2	tablespoons unsalted butter
2	tablespoons chopped chives
4	slices bacon, crisp-fried, crumbled

Arrange the bread slices on a baking sheet. Bake at 350 degrees on center oven rack just until bread begins to crisp. Spread with a mixture of cheese and 1/4 cup butter. Store, covered with plastic wrap, until serving time.

Sauté the sliced apples, onion and garlic in 1/4 cup butter in a large heavy saucepan over medium heat for 5 minutes, stirring occasionally. Add the chicken stock. Simmer for 20 minutes or until the apples are tender. Purée the mixture in 3 batches in a blender or food processor. Combine the purée with the cream and Calvados in a saucepan. Bring to a simmer; season with salt and pepper. May cool at this point and chill overnight. Bring soup to a simmer again before proceeding.

Cut each apple half into 12 thin slices; toss with the lemon juice in a bowl. Sauté the apple slices in 2 tablespoons butter in a large skillet over medium-high heat for 10 minutes or until golden brown.

Broil the croutons 5 inches from heat source for 2 minutes or until the cheese bubbles. Ladle the soup into bowls. Top each serving with 2 red apple slices and 2 Granny Smith apple slices. Sprinkle with chives. Serve with the warm croutons; garnish the croutons with the bacon.

COLD RASPBERRY SOUP

Serves 6

The delicious taste, beautiful presentation and ease of preparation of this soup make it super for a ladies' luncheon.

2　packages frozen raspberries, thawed
1/2　cup sour cream
1/3　cup sugar
2　cups water
1/2　cup dry red wine

Purée the raspberries in a blender. Add the sour cream and sugar; process until smooth. Stir in the water and wine. Spoon into airtight container. Chill overnight. Shake or stir well before serving. Serve cold.

AVGOLEMONO

Serves 6 to 8

Garnish this Greek lemon soup with a thin slice of lemon and a sprig of parsley and serve it with a Greek bread and salad (page 49).

2　quarts strong chicken stock
1/2　cup uncooked rice
3　egg whites
3　egg yolks, beaten
1/4　cup strained lemon juice
　　Salt and pepper to taste

Bring the chicken stock to a boil in a large saucepan. Add the rice gradually. Cook for 20 minutes or until tender; remove from heat. Beat the egg whites in a mixer bowl until stiff peaks form. Add the egg yolks, beating constantly. Add the lemon juice. Add several tablespoons of the chicken stock 1 tablespoon at a time, beating constantly. Stir the tempered egg mixture into the soup. Cook over low heat just until heated through; do not boil. Season with salt and pepper.

BEAN BLANCO ESPECIAL

Serves 8

Serve this soup in bowls lined with flour tortillas. Add shredded Monterey Jack cheese, sliced black olives, chunky salsa, sour cream and chopped avocado.

1	pound dried white beans
5¼	cups chicken broth
1	large white onion, chopped
2	cloves of garlic, minced
1	tablespoon each oregano and cumin
½	teaspoon ground cloves
1	teaspoon salt
1	tablespoon white pepper
1	(7-ounce) can chopped green chilies
1	tablespoon chopped jalapeño pepper (optional)
5	cups chopped cooked chicken breasts
1¾	cups chicken broth

Rinse and sort the beans. Soak in water to cover in a bowl overnight; drain. Combine the beans with 5¼ cups chicken broth, onion, garlic, oregano, cumin, cloves, salt and white pepper in a slow cooker or large saucepan. Cook on Low or simmer for 5 hours or until the beans are tender, stirring occasionally. Stir in the green chilies, jalapeño pepper, chicken and 1¾ cups chicken broth. Cook on Low or simmer for 1 hour. The flavor of this improves when reheated on the second day.

BLACK BEAN CHILI

Serves 12

Serve this hearty soup with bowls of chopped cilantro, sour cream, chopped avocado, shredded cheese and chopped onion for toppings.

1	pound dried black beans
1	(3-pound) pork loin roast
4	cloves of garlic, chopped
3	green chilies, roasted, peeled, chopped
1	medium yellow onion, chopped
2	tablespoons chili powder
1	tablespoon each ground cumin and salt
1	teaspoon oregano
1	(28-ounce) can crushed tomatoes with purée
2	jalapeño peppers, seeded, finely chopped

Rinse and sort the beans. Soak in water to cover in a bowl overnight; drain. Combine the beans with the pork, garlic, green chilies, onion, chili powder, cumin, salt, and oregano in a large saucepan. Add water to cover. Bring to a boil; reduce heat. Simmer, covered, for 6 hours, adding water if needed to cover beans. Remove and shred the pork, discarding the fat and bones. Return the shredded pork to the saucepan with the tomatoes and jalapeño peppers. Cook for 1 hour or until of desired consistency.

BOOKBINDER SOUP

Serves 12 to 16

This soup from The Mayflower Restaurant uses snapper, whitefish or other fresh fish available in season.

1   pound minced clams
    Fresh fish, cut into pieces
1   gallon water
2   cups chopped celery
1   cup chopped carrots
1   cup chopped onion
1   tablespoon beef base
1   teaspoon Worcestershire sauce
1   teaspoon each marjoram, salt and seasoned salt
1/4 teaspoon pepper
1   (12-ounce) can tomato purée
    Roux of 2 tablespoons butter and 2 tablespoons flour
1/4 cup sherry

Combine the clams and fish with the water in a large saucepan. Boil for 15 minutes. Add the celery, carrots, onion, beef base, Worcestershire sauce, marjoram, salt, seasoned salt and pepper. Simmer for 30 minutes. Add the tomato purée. Simmer for 30 minutes. Stir in a roux of melted butter and flour. Cook until thickened, stirring constantly. Adjust the seasonings. Stir in the sherry just before serving.

CHICKEN AND CRAB GUMBO

Serves 20

Serve this hearty cold weather classic with a salad and French bread. Garnish the servings with fresh basil.

1   cup each finely chopped celery and onion
1/2 cup finely chopped leek, white part only
1   cup finely chopped carrots
6   tablespoons butter
1   small can tomato purée
1   medium can chopped tomatoes
1   cup uncooked rice
1   cup dry white wine
16 cups chicken broth
2   cups chopped cooked chicken
1/2 cup cooked crab meat
1   teaspoon gumbo filé
    Celery salt, salt and pepper to taste

Sauté the celery, onion, leek and carrots in the butter in a large saucepan. Add the tomato purée, tomatoes, rice, wine and chicken broth. Bring to a boil; reduce heat. Simmer for 45 minutes or until rice is tender. Add the chicken, crab meat, gumbo filé, celery salt, salt and pepper. Cook until heated through.

CHICKEN AND SAUSAGE GUMBO

Serves 8

The andouille sausage, which can be found in meat specialty shops or in the meat section of a good supermarket, gives this classic gumbo its spicy flavor. Italian sausage could also be used.

1½ teaspoons paprika
1 teaspoon dry mustard
1 teaspoon gumbo filé
1 teaspoon garlic powder
1 teaspoon salt
1½ teaspoons cayenne pepper
2 teaspoons black pepper
1 (3-pound) chicken, cut up
½ cup flour
½ cup vegetable oil
¾ cup chopped onion
¾ cup chopped celery
¾ cup chopped green bell pepper
1½ quarts strong chicken stock
1¾ cups thinly sliced andouille sausage
1 bay leaf
2 cloves of garlic, chopped
2 tablespoons hot pepper sauce
    Cooked rice

Mix the paprika, dry mustard, gumbo filé, garlic powder, salt, cayenne pepper and black pepper in a small bowl. Rinse the chicken and pat it dry. Rub with 4 teaspoons of the seasoning mixture. Combine 2 teaspoons of the seasoning mixture with the flour in a bag. Add the chicken, shaking to coat well. Brown the chicken in heated oil in a large skillet for 3 minutes on each side; drain on paper towels.

Stir the remaining flour mixture into the drippings in the skillet. Cook until brown, stirring constantly. Add the onion, celery and green pepper. Cook for several minutes; remove from the heat.

Bring the chicken broth to a boil in a large heavy saucepan. Whisk in the vegetable mixture. Add the sausage. Cook for 15 minutes, stirring frequently and skimming surface if necessary. Add the chicken, bay leaf, garlic and pepper sauce. Simmer for 40 minutes. Remove and chop the chicken, discarding the skin and bones. Skim excess fat from top of gumbo. Return to the gumbo. Cook until heated through; discard the bay leaf. Serve over cooked rice.

CURRIED BUTTERNUT SQUASH SOUP

Serves 6

The squash and apples combine to evoke the flavors of fall in this soup.

The toasted seeds

Seeds from 2¹/₂ pounds butternut squash
1 tablespoon unsalted butter
Salt to taste

The soup

1 cup chopped onion
2 tablespoons vegetable oil
4 cloves of garlic, finely chopped
2 teaspoons (or to taste) curry powder
1 teaspoon ground cumin
Cayenne pepper to taste
2¹/₂ pounds butternut squash, peeled, cut into halves, thinly sliced
3 cups chicken broth
1 pound tart apples, peeled, chopped
Salt and pepper to taste

Spread the seeds on a double thickness of microwave-safe paper towels. Microwave on High for 3 to 5 minutes or until dry. Cool to room temperature. Sauté the seeds in the butter in a skillet over medium high heat for 2 minutes or until golden brown, stirring constantly. Drain on paper towels. Season with salt.

Sauté the onion in the oil in a large heavy saucepan over medium heat until golden brown. Add the garlic, curry powder, cumin and cayenne pepper. Cook for 30 seconds, stirring constantly. Add the squash, chicken broth, 3 cups water and apples. Simmer, covered, for 25 minutes or until the squash is tender. Purée the mixture in several batches in a blender or food processor. Return to the saucepan and season with salt and pepper. Cook until heated through. Sprinkle the servings with the toasted squash seeds.

ELEGANT MUSHROOM SOUP

Serves 4

This soup is elegant enough to serve to dinner guests. Top the servings with a dollop of Crème Fraîche (page 194) or sour cream and chopped parsley or green onion tops.

1 pound mushrooms, coarsely chopped
4 green onions with tops, coarsely chopped
¹/₂ cup butter
¹/₃ cup flour
¹/₄ teaspoon dry mustard
2 teaspoons salt
Cayenne pepper to taste
¹/₄ teaspoon black pepper
2 cups each chicken broth and whipping cream or half and half
¹/₃ cup sherry (optional)

Sauté the mushrooms and green onions in the butter in a saucepan for 5 minutes. Stir in the flour, dry mustard, salt, cayenne pepper and black pepper. Stir in the chicken broth and cream gradually. Simmer until thickened and smooth, stirring constantly. Add the sherry.

MINESTRONE

Serves 6 to 8

Serve this hearty vegetable-rich soup with a sprinkle of Parmesan cheese and sourdough bread.

1	quart water
1	cup dried Great Northern beans
1	pound Italian sausage
4	ounces bacon, chopped
2	onions, chopped
1	cup sliced celery
1	cup sliced carrots
2	cloves of garlic, chopped
1	large zucchini, sliced
1	cup chopped turnips
1	(16-ounce) can tomatoes
1½	teaspoons basil
1	bay leaf
2	teaspoons salt
¼	teaspoon pepper
4	chicken bouillon cubes
4	cups water
3	cups shredded cabbage
½	cup uncooked macaroni

Bring 1 quart water to a boil in a saucepan; remove from the heat. Add the beans. Let stand for 1 hour or longer.

Brown the sausage with the bacon in a heavy saucepan. Remove and slice the sausage; drain all but 1 tablespoon of the drippings. Return the sausage to the saucepan with the onions, celery, carrots and garlic. Cook for 1 minute, stirring constantly. Add the zucchini, turnips, tomatoes, undrained beans, basil, bay leaf, salt and pepper. Stir in the bouillon cubes dissolved in 4 cups water. Bring to a boil; reduce heat. Simmer for 1 to 1½ hours or until the beans are tender. Stir in the cabbage and macaroni. Cook for 15 minutes longer or until the cabbage and macaroni are tender; discard the bay leaf.

ONION SOUP

Serves 6 to 8

Serve this French classic soup with a salad and bread for a luncheon or supper, or as the first course of an elegant dinner.

1½ pounds onions
3 tablespoons butter
½ teaspoon salt
¼ teaspoon pepper
2 tablespoons flour
4 (15-ounce) cans beef broth
1 tablespoon Cognac
2 cups shredded Swiss, Gruyère or Emmenthaler cheese

Cut the onions into halves lengthwise and then into thin slices. Sauté in the butter in a heavy saucepan over medium heat for 30 to 45 minutes or until carmelized but not burned. Season with salt and pepper. Reduce the heat to medium. Stir in the flour. Cook for 3 minutes or until the flour is light brown, stirring constantly. Add the beef broth. Increase the heat to high. Bring the soup to a boil; reduce the heat to medium. Simmer for 30 minutes. Stir in the Cognac. Ladle into ovenproof soup bowls; sprinkle with the cheese. Broil for several minutes or until the cheese melts.

POTAGE A LA FLORENTINE

Serves 6

This is a popular soup at La Jardiniere Restaurant.

½ cup chopped onion
2 tablespoons butter
1 (10-ounce) package frozen spinach, thawed, drained
5 cups chicken broth
⅓ cup uncooked rice
  Freshly grated nutmeg, salt and pepper to taste
½ cup whipping cream
  Fresh lemon juice

Sauté the onion in the butter in a saucepan for 5 minutes or until tender. Stir in the spinach. Cook, covered, over low heat for 5 minutes, stirring occasionally. Add the chicken broth. Bring to a boil. Stir in the rice, nutmeg, salt and pepper. Simmer, loosely covered, for 20 minutes. Purée in blender or food processor, adding additional chicken broth if needed. Cool to room temperature. Stir in cream and heat to serving temperature. Squeeze fresh lemon juice into bowls just before serving.

POTATO SOUP

Serves 4 to 6

Garnish this with shredded Cheddar cheese for a hearty soup that is particularly inviting during the cold winter season.

6	cups chopped peeled potatoes
1	cup chopped carrots
1	cup chopped celery
1/2	cup chopped onion
2	tablespoons parsley flakes
1	cup chopped cooked ham (optional)
2	(to 3) cups chicken broth
2	teaspoons salt
1/2	cup flour
3	cups milk

Combine the potatoes, carrots, celery, onion, parsley flakes, ham, chicken broth and salt in a 4-quart saucepan. Bring to a boil; reduce the heat. Simmer for 30 minutes. Blend the flour and milk in a small bowl. Add to the soup. Cook until thickened, stirring constantly.

TAFFY APPLE SALAD

Serves 6 to 8

Use both red and green apples for a more colorful salad. Garnish the top with additional peanuts.

1	(16-ounce) can crushed pineapple
4	cups miniature marshmallows
1	tablespoon flour
1/2	cup sugar
1	egg, beaten
1 1/2	tablespoons white vinegar
8	ounces whipped topping
2	(to 3) cups coarsely chopped unpeeled apples
1	cup chopped Spanish peanuts

Drain the pineapple, reserving the juice. Combine the pineapple with the marshmallows in a bowl; set aside.

Combine the reserved juice with the flour, sugar, egg and vinegar in a saucepan; mix well. Cook until slightly thickened, stirring constantly. Cool to room temperature. Fold in the whipped topping, marshmallow mixture, apples and peanuts. Chill for several hours.

BING CHERRY SALAD

Serves 8 to 10

The cashews give this salad an unusual flavor. You could substitute another nut or omit them altogether.

1   large can dark sweet pitted cherries
1   package cherry gelatin
4   ounces cashews (optional)
8   large marshmallows, chopped
2   (to 3) tablespoons mayonnaise-type salad dressing
1   cup whipping cream, whipped, or 1 cup whipped topping

Drain the cherries, reserving the juice. Add enough water to the reserved juice to measure 2 cups. Bring the juice mixture to a boil in a saucepan. Stir in the gelatin until dissolved. Add the cherries and ⅔ of the cashews. Pour into a 9x9-inch dish. Chill for 1 hour or until set.

Combine the remaining cashews, marshmallows, salad dressing and whipped cream in a bowl; mix well. Spread over the congealed layer. Cut into squares to serve.

PEACH SALAD

Serves 10 to 15

Whipping this salad makes it very light and fluffy.

1   (10-ounce) can peaches
1   (3-ounce) package orange gelatin
1   (3-ounce) package lemon gelatin
2   cups boiling water
1   cup orange juice
8   ounces whipped topping

Drain and mash the peaches, reserving the juice. Add enough water to the reserved juice to measure 1 cup. Dissolve the gelatin in the boiling water in a bowl. Stir in the peach juice and orange juice. Chill until set. Whip the gelatin until light and fluffy. Fold in the peaches and whipped topping. Spoon into a 9x13-inch dish. Chill until set. Cut into squares to serve.

GREEK-STYLE BEEF SALAD

Serves 8 to 10

Men really like this great summer salad. Serve it with lettuce in pita rounds or on a bed of lettuce.

The salad

2   pounds thinly sliced cooked roast beef
2   (6-ounce) jars marinated artichoke hearts
1   medium green bell pepper, slivered
1   medium red bell pepper, slivered
1   large red onion, sliced
2   cups sliced black olives
8   ounces feta cheese, crumbled
1   cup minced parsley

The dressing

    Olive oil
1/3 cup red wine vinegar
2   cloves of garlic, minced
1   teaspoon basil
1   teaspoon oregano
1/2 teaspoon tarragon
    Salt and pepper to taste

Cut the roast beef into thin strips. Drain the artichoke hearts, reserving the marinade. Combine the beef and artichokes with the bell peppers, onion, olives, cheese and parsley in a bowl; mix well.

Add enough olive oil to the reserved artichoke marinade to measure 2/3 cup. Combine with the vinegar, garlic, basil, oregano, tarragon, salt and pepper in a small bowl; mix well. Add to the salad. Marinate in the refrigerator overnight.

CHICKEN RICE SALAD WITH ARTICHOKES

Serves 6

The marinated vegetables give this a zippier flavor for a chicken salad with a difference.

1/2 cup sliced artichoke hearts
1   cup chopped celery
1/2 cup chopped green bell pepper
1/2 cup zesty Italian salad dressing
1   (6-ounce) package long grain and wild rice mix
2   whole chicken breasts, cooked, chopped
1/2 cup mayonnaise
8   ounces mushrooms, sliced

Combine the artichoke hearts, celery and green pepper with the salad dressing in a bowl; mix well. Marinate in the refrigerator overnight.

Cook the rice using the package directions and reducing the amount of water by 1/2 cup. Combine the rice with the chicken and mayonnaise in a bowl. Add the mushrooms and marinated vegetables; mix well. Chill until serving time. Serve the salad on lettuce-lined plates.

CHICKEN AND GRAPE SALAD

Serves 6 to 8

Look forward to the salad days of spring and summer with this refreshing chicken salad.

3½   pounds chicken breast filets
4   (or 5) stalks celery, coarsely chopped
1½   cups seedless green grape halves
1½   teaspoons thyme
1½   teaspoons garlic powder
        Salt and freshly ground pepper to taste
2½   (to 3) cups mayonnaise, or enough to bind

Rinse the chicken well. Poach it in water in a saucepan until tender; drain and cool to room temperature. Cut into ¾-inch to 1-inch pieces.

Combine the chicken with the celery and grapes in a large bowl. Add the thyme, garlic powder, salt and pepper. Stir in enough mayonnaise to bind. Chill, covered, for 1 hour or longer.

ASIAN CHICKEN SALAD

Serves 6 to 8

Add fresh fruit and breadsticks to this crunchy salad for a delightful luncheon salad. The ingredients can be prepared early in the day, but it should be assembled at the last minute for the best results.

The marinade

1   tablespoon soy sauce
2   tablespoons salad oil
1   clove of garlic, scored
½   teaspoon grated lemon rind

The salad

2   pounds chicken breast filets
2   tablespoons vegetable oil
3   tablespoons soy sauce
¼   cup lemon juice
½   teaspoon grated lemon rind
1   (10-ounce) package fresh spinach, torn
½   head iceberg lettuce, torn
¼   cup toasted sesame seeds
        Salt to taste
3   cups fresh bean sprouts

Combine the soy sauce, salad oil, garlic clove and lemon rind in a bowl.

Cut the chicken into pieces; rinse and pat dry. Add to the marinade. Marinate, covered, in the refrigerator for several hours.

Sauté the chicken in several batches in the vegetable oil in a skillet for 5 minutes or until cooked through; discard the garlic. Combine the chicken with soy sauce, lemon juice and lemon rind in a bowl. Chill until serving time.

Combine spinach and lettuce in a salad bowl. Sprinkle with the sesame seeds and salt. Add the chicken mixture and bean sprouts; toss lightly to mix well. Serve immediately.

ASIAN CHICKEN SLAW

Serves 8

This is very different from the usual ramen noodle salad. For an even more festive touch, you can add artichoke hearts, water chestnuts and cherry tomatoes.

The dressing

1	cup olive oil
6	tablespoons rice vinegar
1	tablespoon sugar
	Seasoning packets from 2 (3-ounce) packages ramen noodles
1	teaspoon freshly ground pepper

The salad

1/2	head cabbage, finely chopped
1 1/2	heads red leaf lettuce, torn
5	cups chopped cooked chicken
1	red bell pepper, sliced into strips
1	yellow bell pepper, sliced into strips
6	ounces fresh mushrooms, thinly sliced
	Crushed uncooked noodles from 2 (3-ounce) packages ramen noodles
1/4	cup toasted slivered almonds
1/4	cup toasted sesame seeds

Combine the olive oil, rice vinegar, sugar, seasoning packets and pepper in a bowl; mix well.

Combine the cabbage, lettuce, chicken, bell peppers and mushrooms in a salad bowl. Add the dressing; toss to coat well. Top with the ramen noodles, almonds and sesame seeds.

HONEY AND LIME CHICKEN SALAD

Serves 4

The wonderful flavor of this salad is only enhanced by the fact that it uses low-fat ingredients. You may substitute turkey for the chicken.

The dressing

1/3	cup plain low-fat yogurt
1/3	cup low-fat or regular sour cream
2	tablespoons honey
2	teaspoons lime juice
1 1/2	teaspoons finely grated lime rind
1/4	teaspoon salt
1/4	teaspoon pepper

The salad

2	cups chopped cooked chicken breasts
2	medium peaches, peeled, sliced
1	cup seedless red grape halves
1/3	cup thinly sliced celery
2	tablespoons chopped chives

Combine the yogurt, sour cream, honey, lime juice, lime rind, salt and pepper in a small bowl; mix well.

Combine the chicken, peaches, grapes, celery and chives in a salad bowl. Add the dressing; mix gently. Chill, covered, for 1 to 24 hours.

SUMMERTIME SEA SHELL SALAD

Serves 8

White water rafters are served this refreshing salad when they break for lunch along the New River in West Virginia.

The dressing

1	(6-ounce) can frozen orange juice concentrate, thawed
1	tablespoon honey
1	tablespoon basil
1	clove of garlic, minced
	Nutmeg to taste
1/2	teaspoon salt
1/2	teaspoon pepper
1/2	cup safflower oil

The salad

16	ounces uncooked medium shell pasta
1	(16-ounce) can mandarin oranges, drained
1	(16-ounce) can pineapple chunks, drained
1	cup thawed frozen peas
1	cup sliced carrots
1	cup cashews
2	cups julienned cooked ham or chicken

Combine the orange juice concentrate, honey, basil, garlic, nutmeg, salt and pepper in a blender container; process until smooth. Add the oil gradually, processing constantly until thick.

Cook the pasta using package directions just until tender; rinse with cold water and drain. Combine with the oranges, pineapple, peas, carrots, cashews and ham in a large bowl. Add the dressing to the salad; toss to coat well. Chill for 1 hour or longer.

CHICKEN WALDORF

Serves 6

Just add chicken to this upscale version of the classic Waldorf salad to serve it as the main dish at a luncheon or summer supper.

1	cup mayonnaise or plain yogurt
2	tablespoons Dijon mustard
1	tablespoon brown sugar
5	cups chopped cooked chicken
2	large unpeeled apples, chopped
1	cup thinly sliced celery
1/2	cup chopped walnuts
1/4	cup raisins (optional)

Combine the mayonnaise, mustard and brown sugar in a bowl; mix until smooth. Fold in the chicken, apples, celery, walnuts and raisins. Chill for 2 to 6 hours.

WON TON CHICKEN SALAD

Serves 8

The pickled onions give this crunchy salad a different flavor.

The dressing

6	tablespoons sugar
1/4	cup vinegar
1/2	cup corn oil
1	tablespoon sesame oil
1	teaspoon salt
1/2	teaspoon pepper

The salad

8	ounces won ton skins
	Oil for deep frying
6	chicken breast filets, cooked, shredded
4	scallions, thinly sliced
1	cup thinly sliced sweet pickled onions
1	small head lettuce, torn
1/2	cup toasted slivered almonds
3	tablespoons toasted sesame seeds

Mix the sugar, vinegar, corn oil, sesame oil, salt and pepper in a jar with cover.

Deep-fry the won ton skins in oil in deep-fryer; drain and crumble. Combine with the chicken, scallions, pickled onions, lettuce, almonds and sesame seeds in a salad bowl; mix well. Add the dressing; toss to coat well. Serve immediately.

MARINATED SALMON SALAD

Serves 12

This salad from Chef Philippe Forcioli of Cafe Patóu can also be served as an appetizer on small buttered toasts, garnished with capers, or with asparagus and a drizzle of olive oil and lemon juice, garnished with parsley.

The salmon

1	(4-pound) salmon filet
4	bay leaves
3	ounces fresh basil
4	sprigs of fresh thyme
1	sprig of fresh rosemary
2	cups sea salt
1	cup packed brown sugar
1	cup each lemon juice and dry white wine
1/4	cup black peppercorns

The salad

Mixed greens
Vinaigrette

Place the salmon skin side down in the larger of 2 shallow pans or fish poacher with tray. Sprinkle with a mixture of the bay leaves, basil, thyme and rosemary. Sprinkle with the sea salt and brown sugar. Pour lemon juice and wine over the top; sprinkle with the peppercorns. Place the second pan on the salmon and weigh it down with a heavy object. Marinate in the refrigerator for 72 hours. Remove from the marinade and slice thinly on the diagonal.

Toss the mixed greens with vinaigrette in a salad bowl. Top with the marinated salmon.

SMOKED SALMON CAESAR SALAD

Serves 12

Jeffrey R. Wells of the City Club of Rockford shares this recipe. He says that the best Caesar salad has a combination of perfect ingredients: a good dressing, an excellent quality cheese, crisp romaine and delicious croutons. This one also has smoked fresh salmon.

The croutons

4	large slices 2-day old French bread or 1/3 baguette
1	large clove of garlic, sliced
2	tablespoons light olive oil
2	tablespoons vegetable oil

The dressing

1	tablespoon red wine vinegar
1	tablespoon minced anchovy (optional)
2	tablespoons Dijon mustard
4	teaspoons minced garlic
3/4	teaspoon freshly ground pepper
1	cup extra-virgin olive and/or pure olive oil
1/4	cup fresh lemon juice
	Worcestershire sauce to taste

The salad

3	heads romaine lettuce
1/2	cup grated Parmesan and/or Romano cheese
3	(or 4) ounces smoked salmon, crumbled

Cut the bread into cubes, leaving the crust on; measure 2 cups cubes. Sauté the garlic in the heated olive oil and vegetable oil in a skillet for 3 minutes or until light brown. Remove the garlic with a slotted spoon. Add the bread cubes to the skillet. Sauté over medium heat until golden brown on all sides, stirring frequently. Drain on paper towels.

Combine the vinegar, anchovy, mustard, garlic and pepper in a bowl. Whisk in the olive oil drop by drop. Whisk in the lemon juice and Worcestershire sauce. Add salt to taste if anchovy is omitted.

Remove the outer green leaves of the romaine lettuce. Tear the inner leaves into 2-inch pieces. Rinse and dry it well. Combine with half the cheese and the croutons in a salad bowl; toss to mix well. Add the remaining cheese and dressing; toss to coat well. Top with the salmon. Serve immediately.

CHARBROILED SHRIMP CAESAR SALAD

Serves 2

The shrimp

The salad

This recipe comes from Cliffbreakers Restaurant.

12 jumbo shrimp, peeled
    Caesar salad dressing

    Romaine lettuce, torn
    Sliced red onion
    Sliced mushrooms
    Caesar salad dressing
    Tomato wedges
    Croutons

Thread the shrimp onto 2 skewers; place in a shallow dish. Drizzle with the salad dressing. Marinate in the refrigerator overnight. Grill the shrimp for 2 minutes on each side or until firm.

Combine the romaine lettuce, onion, mushrooms and salad dressing in a salad bowl. Place in 2 serving bowls. Top each with a skewer of shrimp, tomato wedges and croutons.

BOW TIE SPINACH SALAD

Serves 8 to 10

The dressing

The salad

Combine the best of pasta and spinach salads with a zesty dressing for a salad that is pretty as well as tasty.

3/4 cup olive oil or vegetable oil
3/4 cup white wine vinegar
3 cloves of garlic, crushed
2 teaspoons Dijon mustard
1/2 cup grated Parmesan cheese
1 tablespoon minced fresh oregano or 1 teaspoon dried oregano
    Salt and pepper to taste

1 (16-ounce) package bow tie pasta, cooked, drained
1 package spinach, torn
3 tomatoes, chopped
1/2 cup sliced green onions
1/2 cup sliced black olives
3/4 cup crumbled feta cheese

Combine the olive oil, vinegar, garlic, mustard, Parmesan cheese, oregano, salt and pepper in a bowl; mix well.

Combine the pasta, spinach, tomatoes, green onion, olives and feta cheese in a salad bowl. Add the salad dressing; toss to coat well. Chill until serving time.

CAESAR PASTA PRIMAVERA

Serves 4 to 6

Add 1½ cups cooked chicken, turkey or ham for a summer lunch or light dinner. Combine green, red and yellow bell peppers for a colorful touch.

4	cups uncooked tri-colored pasta
2	tablespoons olive oil
2	cups broccoli flowerets
1	cup chopped red bell pepper
½	cup chopped red onion
½	cup each garbanzo beans and sliced pitted black olives
4	slices bacon, crisp-fried, crumbled
½	(to 1) cup grated Parmesan cheese
1	bottle of Caesar salad dressing

Cook the pasta using package directions; rinse in cold water and drain. Toss with the olive oil in a bowl. Chill in the refrigerator. Steam the broccoli for 2 minutes. Rinse with cold water and drain. Combine with the bell pepper, onion, beans and olives in a bowl. Chill in the refrigerator. Add the pasta, bacon, cheese and salad dressing just before serving; toss to coat well.

PICNIC PASTA SALAD

Serves 10

Basil fresh from the garden is very good in this salad. Chopped cooked chicken can be added for a main-dish salad.

The dressing

⅔	cup olive oil
	Juice of 1 lemon
1	tablespoon Dijon mustard
1	clove of garlic, crushed
¼	cup red wine vinegar
1	cup chopped fresh basil leaves
½	teaspoon cayenne pepper

The salad

1	(16-ounce) package rotini, cooked, drained
2	(6-ounce) jars marinated artichoke hearts
1	can hearts of palm, drained, sliced
5	ounces green olives, sliced, drained
2	tomatoes, chopped
1	avocado, chopped
4	green onions, chopped
3	ounces capers

Combine the olive oil, lemon juice, mustard, garlic, vinegar, basil and cayenne pepper in a bowl; mix well. Let stand for 1 hour.

Combine the pasta, undrained artichokes, hearts of palm, olives, tomatoes, avocado, green onions and capers in a salad bowl; mix gently. Add the salad dressing; toss lightly to coat well.

WALNUT AND AVOCADO SALAD

Serves 8

The smooth taste of the avocado, the crunch of the walnuts and the zesty flavor of the dressing make this a very special green salad.

The dressing

1/3	cup white wine vinegar
1/2	teaspoon lemon juice
2/3	cup vegetable oil
1	clove of garlic, minced
1	teaspoon salt
1/4	teaspoon pepper

The salad

1/2	head each iceberg and romaine lettuce, torn
1	avocado, chopped
1/2	cup toasted walnuts

Combine the vinegar, lemon juice, oil, garlic, salt and pepper in a dressing cruet; mix well. Chill for 2 to 24 hours.

Combine the lettuces, avocado and walnuts in a salad bowl. Drizzle with the desired amount of salad dressing; toss to coat well. Serve immediately.

MEXICAN BEAN SALAD

Serves 12

Serve this colorful low-fat salad with a Mexican buffet or take it to a potluck supper.

The dressing

2	tablespoons seasoned rice vinegar
2	tablespoons cider vinegar
	Juice of 1 lime
2	cloves of garlic, minced
1	jalapeño pepper, minced
2	teaspoons ground cumin
1	teaspoon ground coriander
1/2	teaspoon salt

The salad

2	(15-ounce) cans black beans, drained
2	cups frozen corn, thawed
1	tomato, chopped
1	green bell pepper, chopped
1	red or yellow bell pepper, chopped
1	cup chopped jicama
1/2	cup thinly sliced green onions
3/4	cup chopped fresh cilantro

Combine the vinegars, lime juice, garlic, jalapeño pepper, cumin, coriander and salt in a covered jar; shake to mix well.

Combine the beans, corn, tomato, bell peppers, jicama, green onions and cilantro in a large salad bowl; mix well. Add the salad dressing; toss to coat well. Chill until serving time.

BROCCOLI SALAD

Serves 6 to 8

An easy and colorful salad which can be varied with the addition of cauliflower, cashews or your family's favorite extras.

1	cup mayonnaise
1/4	cup sugar
2	tablespoons white vinegar
2	large bunches broccoli
1	medium red onion, coarsely chopped
1	cup sunflower seeds
12	slices bacon, crisp-fried, crumbled
1/2	cup raisins
2	cups shredded Cheddar cheese

Combine the mayonnaise, sugar and vinegar in a bowl; mix well. Cut the broccoli into bite-sized pieces. Combine with the onion, sunflower seeds, bacon, raisins and cheese in a salad bowl. Add the dressing just before serving; toss to coat well.

ORIENTAL COLESLAW

Serves 6 to 8

This is especially good with seafood, or add chopped cooked chicken for a luncheon main dish. Even children like the crunch of the noodles.

1/3	cup olive oil
3	tablespoons red wine vinegar
2	tablespoons sugar
1	package oriental-flavor ramen noodles
1/2	head cabbage, shredded
3	(to 6) green onions, sliced
2	tablespoons toasted sesame seeds
1/2	cup toasted slivered almonds

Combine the olive oil, vinegar, sugar and seasoning packet from the noodles in a bowl; mix well. Chill until serving time. Combine the cabbage, green onions, sesame seeds and almonds in a serving bowl. Crush the noodles and add to the salad with the dressing; toss to coat well.

GREEK SALAD

Serves 6 to 8

Always use olive oil and fresh lemon juice for an authentic Greek salad, which is known as a meal in itself. Just add crusty bread and white wine for a super lunch.

The vinaigrette

1/3	cup olive oil
2	tablespoons fresh lemon juice
3	tablespoons red or white wine vinegar
1	teaspoon sugar
1	clove of garlic, minced
1 1/2	teaspoons fresh oregano or 1/2 teaspoon dried oregano
1/4	teaspoon pepper

The salad

5	cups torn mixed salad greens such as red leaf lettuce, endive or romaine
1	medium tomato, chopped
1/2	cucumber, seeded, sliced
1/2	red onion, sliced
1/2	cup sliced radishes, (optional)
1	cup Kalamata or Greek olives
1	cup crumbled feta cheese
	Oregano to taste
	Chives to taste
	Pepperoncini to taste

Combine the olive oil, lemon juice, vinegar, sugar, garlic, oregano and pepper in a bowl; mix well. Chill until serving time or for up to 2 weeks.

Combine the salad greens, tomato, cucumber, onion, radishes, olives and cheese in a salad bowl. Chill for up to 2 hours. Stir the vinaigrette. Add to the salad; toss to coat well. Sprinkle with oregano, chives and pepperoncini.

BLEU CHEESE SALAD

Serves 4 or 5

The most avid lover of bleu cheese will be satisfied to find bleu cheese in both the salad and the dressing in this delicious recipe. You can also add tomatoes and mushrooms.

The dressing

3/4	cup vegetable oil
1/4	cup balsamic vinegar
1/4	cup white wine vinegar
2	ounces bleu cheese, crumbled
1/3	cup sugar
1	clove of garlic
1/2	teaspoon salt

The salad

1	head romaine lettuce, torn
1/4	red onion, sliced
4	slices bacon, crisp-fried, crumbled
2	ounces bleu cheese, crumbled
2	tablespoons toasted sesame seeds

Combine the oil, vinegars, bleu cheese, sugar, garlic and salt in the blender container; process until smooth.

Combine the romaine, onion, bacon, bleu cheese and sesame seeds in a salad bowl. Drizzle with the desired amount of dressing; toss to coat well.

SESAME SPINACH SALAD

Serves 6 to 8

Our absolute favorite spinach salad!

The dressing

1/3	cup vegetable oil
3	tablespoons fresh lemon juice
2	tablespoons soy sauce
2	tablespoons toasted sesame seeds

The salad

8	ounces fresh mushrooms, thickly sliced
1/2	cup Italian salad dressing
1	pound fresh spinach, torn
1	cup fresh bean sprouts
6	slices bacon, crisp-fried, crumbled

Combine the oil, lemon juice, soy sauce and sesame seeds in a jar; mix well.

Combine the mushrooms with the Italian salad dressing in a salad bowl; mix well. Marinate for 1 hour. Add the spinach and bean sprouts. Drizzle with the oil and lemon juice dressing; toss to coat well. Sprinkle with the bacon. Serve immediately.

GERMAN POTATO SALAD

Serves 10

Even people who claim not to care for German potato salad enjoyed this one! The unpeeled potatoes give it a new twist.

1½ (to 2) pounds small new potatoes
2 (to 4) green onions, sliced
4 ounces bacon, chopped
1 tablespoon sugar
1 tablespoon flour
¼ teaspoon celery seeds
1 teaspoon salt
¼ teaspoon pepper
¼ cup cider vinegar
½ cup water

Cook the unpeeled potatoes, covered, in water to partially cover in a large saucepan over low heat for 25 minutes or until tender. Drain and cool slightly. Cut into quarters. Combine with the green onions in a salad bowl.

Fry the bacon in a skillet. Remove the bacon with a slotted spoon and drain all but 1 tablespoon of the drippings. Stir in the sugar, flour, celery seeds, salt and pepper. Cook for 1 minute, stirring constantly. Add the vinegar and water. Cook for 1 minute or until thickened, stirring constantly. Add to the salad with the bacon; mix gently. Serve warm or at room temperature.

SAUERKRAUT SALAD

Serves 6 to 8

A very heart-healthy salad to keep in the refrigerator for up to one week.

1 (2-pound) package sauerkraut
1 cup finely chopped celery
½ cup finely chopped onion
1 green bell pepper, finely chopped
1 (4-ounce) jar chopped pimento, drained
⅓ cup vinegar
1½ cups sugar
  Salt and pepper to taste

Combine the sauerkraut, celery, onion, green pepper and pimento in a bowl with a lid. Add the vinegar, sugar, salt and pepper; mix well. Chill, covered, in the refrigerator overnight.

Entrées

Barbecued Beef Brisket, 55	Lemon-Basil Grilled Chicken, 70
Brazilian Pot Roast, 55	Grilled Teriyaki Chicken, 71
Red Wine Pot Roast, 56	Jambalaya, 71
Never-Fail Prime Rib, 56	Monterey Chicken, 72
Beef in Brew, 56	Chicken Piccata, 72
Lazy Beef Casserole, 57	Roquefort and Lemon Chicken, 73
Beef at its Best, 57	Ratatouille with Chicken and Pesto, 73
Individual Beef Wellingtons, 58	Sesame and Ginger Chicken, 74
Venetian Venison Picante, 58	Spicy Thai-Style Chicken and Rice, 74
Shish Kabobs, 59	Tarragon Chicken Breasts, 75
Veal Cutlets with Brie and Basil, 59	Chicken Vesuvio and Potatoes, 75
Veal Chops, 60	Rock Cornish Hens, 76
Stuffed Veal Chops, 60	Cornish Hens, 76
Crown Roast of Pork with Stuffing, 61	Turkey with Raisins and Capers, 77
Luau Pork Roast, 62	Duck Breast with Port Sauce, 78
Chinese Pork Tenderloin, 62	Fish Stew Provençale, 79
Pork Roast with Peppercorn Crust, 63	Orange Roughy with Mushroom Sauce, 80
Marinated Pork Tenderloin, 63	Red Snapper a l'Orange, 80
Barbecued Country Pork Ribs, 64	Grilled Salmon, 81
Oven-Barbecued Spareribs, 64	Salmon Steaks with Dill and Capers, 81
Paella, 65	Herbed Shrimp de Jonghe, 82
Ham Braised in Madeira, 66	Mustard Broiled Shrimp, 82
Indonesian Saté, 66	Risotto with Shrimp, 83
Perfect Roast Leg of Lamb, 67	Spicy Baked Shrimp, 83
Mediterranean Lamb Chops, 67	Shrimp and Vegetables en Croute, 84
Lamb Stew Over Rice, 68	Cioppino, 84
Almond Lemon Chicken, 69	Seafood Stir-Fry, 85
Ginger Chicken, 70	Seafood Coquilles, 85

BARBECUED BEEF BRISKET

Serves 10

The brisket is very tender when cooked with this very easy but tasty recipe. Serve the leftovers for sandwiches.

1   (4 to 6-pound) beef brisket
2   teaspoons salt
1/2 teaspoon pepper
2   medium onions, sliced
4   stalks celery, sliced
1   (12-ounce) bottle of chili sauce
1   cup water
1   (12-ounce) can beer

Wine Suggestion
Gamay Beaujolais

Place the brisket in a large shallow roasting pan; sprinkle with salt and pepper. Place the onions and celery on top. Pour a combination of chili sauce and water into the pan. Bake, covered, at 300 degrees for 3 hours, adding additional water if needed. Stir in the beer. Bake, covered, for 1½ to 2 hours longer or until very tender, basting occasionally. Slice the brisket cross grain. Serve with the cooking sauce.

BRAZILIAN POT ROAST

Serves 6

Border this roast with glazed orange slices and crisp parsley and serve it with buttered noodles or new potatoes.

3   slices bacon
1   (4-pound) lean round or rump roast
2   tablespoons lemon juice
1   teaspoon salt
1   clove of garlic, minced
2/3 cup chopped onion
1/4 cup chopped parsley
1   teaspoon sugar
1   cup canned tomatoes or 3 small tomatoes, chopped
1/2 bay leaf
4   whole cloves
1/2 teaspoon cinnamon
1   cup orange juice

Wine Suggestion
Petit Sirah

Fry the bacon in a heavy Dutch oven until crisp; remove and crumble bacon, reserving the drippings in the pan. Sprinkle the roast with lemon juice and salt. Add to the drippings. Cook until evenly brown on all sides. Add the bacon, garlic, onion, parsley, sugar, tomatoes, bay leaf, cloves and cinnamon. Bring to a boil; reduce heat. Simmer, covered, for 10 minutes. Add the orange juice. Simmer, covered, for 3 hours or until very tender, turning the roast several times and adding water if needed. Remove the roast to a serving plate. Skim fat off the pan juices, discarding the bay leaf; serve with the roast. You may bake this in the oven if you prefer.

RED WINE POT ROAST

Serves 6 to 8

It is great to come home to the luscious smell of this easy "no-hands-on" dinner all ready to serve.

1   (4 to 5-pound) pot roast, trimmed
1   (10-ounce) can cream of mushroom soup
3/4 cup dry red wine
1   envelope onion soup mix

Wine Suggestion
California Merlot

Line a roasting pan with heavy-duty foil. Place the roast in the prepared pan. Mix the soup, wine and soup mix in a bowl. Pour over the roast; seal the foil tightly. Roast at 250 degrees for 5 hours.

NEVER-FAIL PRIME RIB

Serves 5 to 6

Nothing could be simpler or more elegant than this recipe for prime rib. The roast will be crisp and very brown on the outside and pink all the way through.

1   prime rib roast of at least 2 ribs
     Salt and pepper to taste

Wine Suggestion
Cabernet Sauvignon

Let the roast stand at room temperature for 1 hour. Sprinkle with salt and pepper; place fat side up in a shallow roasting pan. Roast at 375 degrees for 1 hour; turn off the oven. Do not open the oven door. Let the roast stand in the closed oven for 3 hours or longer. Set the oven temperature to 375 degrees. Roast for 30 to 40 minutes longer. Cut into thin slices.

BEEF IN BREW

Serves 4 to 6

Turn an inexpensive cut of meat into a tender treat with this marinade. Serve it with baked potatoes, a green salad and garlic bread for a great summer dinner.

1   (12-ounce) can beer
1/2 cup soy sauce
1/2 cup vegetable oil
1   (or 2) cloves of garlic, minced
1/8 teaspoon pepper
1   boneless chuck steak

Wine Suggestion
Gamay Beaujolais

Combine the beer, soy sauce, oil, garlic and pepper in a 9x13-inch dish. Add the steak, turning to coat well. Marinate, covered, in the refrigerator for 8 to 24 hours, turning several times. Grill the steak until done to taste.

LAZY BEEF CASSEROLE

Serves 4

What could be better than a heart-healthy low-fat recipe that is also easy to make? Serve it with rice or noodles and a salad for a complete meal.

1   pound lean beef chuck
1/2 cup red wine
1   (10-ounce) can beef consommé
1   medium onion, chopped
1/4 teaspoon rosemary
     Freshly ground pepper to taste
1/4 cup fine dry bread crumbs
1/4 cup flour

Wine Suggestion
Petit Sirah

Cut the chuck into 1½-inch cubes. Combine with the wine, consommé, onion, rosemary and pepper in a baking dish. Mix the bread crumbs with the flour in a bowl. Stir into the beef mixture. Bake, covered, at 300 degrees for 3 hours or at a lower temperature until cooked through.

BEEF AT ITS BEST

Serves 4

Put apples in to bake with this stew and dessert will be ready when you are. Just add a green salad and French bread for an easy dinner. The flavor improves, as it does with most stews, when reheated the next day.

2   pounds lean beef stew meat
1½   teaspoons sugar
1   cup apple cider
1   (10-ounce) can beef broth
1   bay leaf
2/3   teaspoon whole allspice
1½   teaspoons salt
4   carrots, cut into 2-inch pieces
4   small onions, cut into quarters
      Cornstarch
1/2   cup water

Wine Suggestion
Red Rhone-style
wine such as
Cateauneuf du Pape

Trim the fat from the stew meat. Render the fat in a Dutch oven over high heat; discard the fat. Sprinkle the beef with sugar. Brown in the prepared Dutch oven. Add the cider, beef broth, bay leaf, allspice and salt. Bring to a boil. Add the carrots and onions; cover. Bring to a simmer. Bake at 350 degrees for 2 to 2½ hours or until tender; discard the bay leaf. Thicken with a mixture of cornstarch and water. Serve immediately or place in the refrigerator overnight and reheat the next day.

INDIVIDUAL BEEF WELLINGTONS

Serves 4

Serve these elegant filets in puff pastry with Béarnaise sauce. Recipe compliments of John Nolte.

4   (6-ounce) filet mignons
     Garlic powder, salt and pepper to taste
1   tablespoon butter
1   sheet frozen puff pastry, thawed
1   ounce pâté or 1/3 cup sautéed mushrooms
1   egg white, slightly beaten

Wine Suggestion
Merlot

Season the beef with garlic powder, salt and pepper. Sauté in the butter in a heavy skillet for 3 minutes on each side. Roll the puff pastry on a floured surface; cut into quarters. Spread 1 side of each filet with pâté or mushrooms. Place pâté side down on pastry. Fold the pastry over the filets, enclosing completely; trim off any excess pastry. Place on a lightly greased baking sheet; brush with the egg white. Bake at 400 degrees for 15 minutes.

VENETIAN VENISON PICANTE

Serves 6

Sheriff Don Gaspirini recommends fried potatoes or rice, a green salad and a hearty bread to complete the menu for a good fall and winter dish.

The marinade

1/2 cup olive oil
1/4 cup wine vinegar
3   cloves of garlic, sliced
1/4 teaspoon salt
1/2 teaspoon pepper

The venison

6   venison filets or 1 (2-pound) venison filet
3   eggs, beaten
2   cups seasoned bread crumbs
1/2 cup olive oil
1   (16-ounce) can stewed tomatoes
1   bay leaf
3   cloves of garlic, sliced
2   tablespoons butter or margarine

Wine Suggestion
Pinot Noir

Combine the olive oil, vinegar, garlic, salt and pepper in a bowl.

Add the venison. Marinate in the refrigerator overnight; drain. Dip the venison into the eggs and coat with the bread crumbs. Fry in the heated olive oil in a skillet over medium heat, turning to brown on both sides.

Remove the venison to a baking dish. Add a mixture of the tomatoes, bay leaf and garlic. Dot with butter. Bake at 325 degrees for 20 minutes. Discard the bay leaf.

SHISH KABOBS

Serves 6

This requires some advance preparation, but it cooks on the grill or in the broiler in just a few minutes and provides the basis for a great cookout or company dinner. Just add rice and a salad of mixed greens and dinner is ready.

The marinade

1/3	cup vegetable oil
1/4	cup red wine
1/4	cup soy sauce
1/4	cup minced onion
1	clove of garlic, minced
1	tablespoon Dijon mustard
1/4	teaspoon oregano
1/4	teaspoon basil
1/4	teaspoon thyme

The shish kabob

2	pounds sirloin steak
12	pieces each green bell pepper, onion and zucchini
12	each cherry tomatoes and mushrooms

Wine Suggestion
Cabernet Sauvignon

Combine the oil, wine, soy sauce, onion, garlic, mustard, oregano, basil and thyme in a bowl or zipper-style plastic food storage bag.

Cut the steak into 1-inch to 1½-inch cubes. Add to the marinade. Marinate in the refrigerator for 4 hours to overnight, turning or stirring several times; drain.

Thread the steak onto 6 skewers, alternating with the green pepper, onion, zucchini, cherry tomatoes and mushrooms. Grill or broil for 10 to 12 minutes or until done to taste, turning frequently.

VEAL CUTLETS WITH BRIE AND BASIL

Serves 6

This dish is light and easy to prepare but provides an elegant entrée with a different flavor.

6	veal cutlets
1/3	cup flour
	Salt to taste
3	tablespoons butter
4	ounces Brie cheese
6	fresh basil leaves
1/2	cup water
1/8	teaspoon salt

Wine Suggestion
French Meursault

Pound the veal cutlets 1/16 inch thick on waxed paper. Coat with a mixture of flour and salt to taste. Brown on both sides in the butter in a 12-inch skillet over medium-high heat. Remove the cutlets to an ovenproof platter. Cut the cheese into 6 portions. Place 1 basil leaf and 1 portion of cheese on half of each cutlet; fold the cutlet over to cover the cheese. Cover the platter with foil. Bake at 350 degrees for 10 to 15 minutes or just until the cheese melts. Add the water and 1/8 teaspoon salt to the skillet, stirring to deglaze. Cook until heated through. Serve over the cutlets.

VEAL CHOPS

Serves 6

This recipe is from Jake Cason of Maria's Italian Restaurant, one of Rockford's oldest and best-known Italian restaurants.

1	cup green bell pepper strips
1	medium onion, thinly sliced
1	clove of garlic, minced
1/4	cup margarine
1	(16-ounce) can tomatoes in purée
1	(6-ounce) can tomato paste
2	ounces anchovy filets, drained, chopped
1/2	cup coarsely chopped black olives
6	veal chops
2	tablespoons margarine
	Salt and pepper to taste

Sauté the green pepper, onion and garlic in 1/4 cup margarine in a medium saucepan until wilted. Stir in the tomatoes, tomato paste, anchovies and olives. Spread in a shallow 3-quart baking dish. Brown the veal chops in 2 tablespoons margarine in a large skillet over high heat. Sprinkle with salt and pepper. Remove to prepared baking dish. Bake at 375 degrees for 45 minutes or until tender.

STUFFED VEAL CHOPS

Serves 2

Men love this dish. It is good served with green noodles and is festive enough for a party.

2	veal rib or loin chops
2	slices Muenster or mozzarella cheese
2	slices prosciutto
2	tablespoons grated Parmesan cheese
	Flour
1	egg, beaten
2	tablespoons each butter and vegetable oil
6	(to 8) mushrooms
1	(to 2) ounces vermouth or dry white wine
1	teaspoon chopped parsley
1/4	cup chicken broth
1/4	cup beef broth
3	tablespoons melted butter
	Salt and pepper to taste

Wine Suggestion Amarone

Cut a horizontal pocket in each veal chop; pound lightly with a meat mallet. Place 1 slice of cheese, 1 slice of prosciutto and 1 tablespoon of Parmesan cheese into each pocket. Coat the chops with flour and dip into egg. Brown the chops in a mixture of 2 tablespoons butter and the oil in a large ovenproof skillet for 2 minutes. Turn the chops and cook for 1 minute longer. Bake at 400 degrees for 15 minutes. Add the mushrooms. Bake for 5 minutes longer; drain. Combine the vermouth, parsley, broths, 3 tablespoons butter, salt and pepper in a measuring cup; mix well. Pour into the skillet. Simmer for 3 to 5 minutes or until heated through.

CROWN ROAST OF PORK WITH STUFFING

Serves 12 to 16

Oh so elegant and yet so simple! This is definitely holiday fare. Serve it with extra stuffing baked in a separate dish, fruit and crusty bread.

The stuffing

1	pound sweet Italian sausage
1/2	cup water
2	tablespoons vegetable oil
4	cups finely chopped onions
2	cups finely chopped carrots
2	cups finely chopped celery
2	cloves of garlic, crushed
7	medium potatoes, peeled, chopped
1/2	teaspoon salt
1/3	cup chopped parsley
1	teaspoon fennel seeds, crushed
3/4	teaspoon salt
1/8	teaspoon pepper

The roast

1	(7 to 8-pound) 16-rib crown roast of pork
1	tablespoon vegetable oil
	Salt and pepper to taste

Wine Suggestion
Italian Amarone

Cut the sausage into halves lengthwise, discarding the casing. Cook in the water in a skillet until the sausage is brown and water has evaporated, stirring with a wooden spoon to break up the sausage. Remove with wooden spoon to drain; cut into small pieces. Add the oil to the drippings in the skillet. Sauté the onions, carrots, celery and garlic in the oil for 15 to 20 minutes or until the carrots are tender. Cook the potatoes with 1/2 teaspoon salt in water to cover in a medium saucepan over high heat for 20 minutes or until tender; drain. Combine the sausage, potatoes, sautéed vegetables, parsley, fennel seeds, 3/4 teaspoon salt and pepper in a large bowl; mix well.

Brush the roast with the oil and sprinkle it with salt and pepper to taste. Wrap the bones with foil to prevent burning. Insert a meat thermometer into the center of loin, taking care not to touch the bone. Place in a shallow roasting pan. Roast at 475 degrees for 15 minutes. Reduce the oven temperature to 325 degrees. Roast for 1 1/2 hours longer. Spoon the stuffing into the center of roast, mounding slightly. Wrap the remaining stuffing in foil. Roast the pork and bake the leftover stuffing for 45 to 60 minutes longer or until pork registers 170 degrees on meat thermometer. Serve with the stuffing.

LUAU PORK ROAST

Serves 10

A great company dish! The roast can be prepared in advance and marinated for up to twenty-four hours.

1	(4-pound) boned pork shoulder roast
1/2	cup pineapple juice
1/2	cup vegetable oil
1/2	cup dark corn syrup
1/4	cup lime juice
1	small clove of garlic, crushed
2	tablespoons brown sugar
1	tablespoon prepared mustard
1	tablespoon soy sauce
1	teaspoon coriander
1/2	teaspoon ginger
2	teaspoons salt

Wine Suggestion
California
Chardonnay

Trim the excess fat from the roast; place in a shallow dish or plastic food storage bag. Combine the pineapple juice, oil, corn syrup, lime juice, garlic, brown sugar, mustard, soy sauce, coriander, ginger and salt in a bowl; mix well. Pour over the roast; cover securely or seal bag. Marinate in the refrigerator for 8 to 24 hours, turning occasionally. Drain, reserving the marinade.

Place the roast fat side up on a rack in a shallow roasting pan; insert a meat thermometer into the thickest part of the roast, taking care not to touch the bone. Roast at 325 degrees for 2 1/2 hours or to 170 degrees on the meat thermometer, basting occasionally with the reserved marinade.

CHINESE PORK TENDERLOIN

Serves 12

The marinade in this recipe is enough to marinate three or four tenderloins, or enough to serve at your next patio party.

3	tablespoons honey
1/4	cup soy sauce
2	tablespoons dry sherry
1/4	cup hoisin sauce
2	tablespoons brown bean sauce
2	(or 3) slices fresh ginger, crushed
2	cloves of garlic, crushed
3	(12 to 15-ounce) pork tenderloins

Combine the honey, soy sauce, wine, hoisin sauce, bean sauce, ginger and garlic in a shallow dish. Trim the silver membrane from the pork; add pork to the marinade. Marinate at room temperature for 2 to 3 hours; drain. Grill the pork until cooked through.

PORK ROAST WITH PEPPERCORN CRUST

Serves 10

Serve with a casserole of wild rice fruited with currants or raisins for a special-occasion dinner.

The roast

1	(4½-pound) boneless pork roast, tied
	Salt to taste
4½	tablespoons unsalted butter, softened
3	tablespoons flour
½	cup each whole black, white, pink and green peppercorns, coarsely crushed

The gravy

¼	cup flour
¼	cup strained roast drippings
1¾	cups chicken broth
1	cup water
2	tablespoons red wine vinegar or to taste
	Salt to taste

Wine Suggestions
Califoirnia Pinot
Noir or Zinfandel

Sprinkle the roast with salt to taste. Blend the butter and flour in a small bowl. Spread the mixture over the top of the roast. Sprinkle the peppercorns over the roast, pressing them lightly into the coating. Place the roast on a rack in a roasting pan. Roast at 450 degrees on the center oven rack for 30 minutes. Reduce the oven temperature to 325 degrees. Roast for 1½ hours longer or to 155 degrees on a meat thermometer. Remove to a cutting board; let stand for 10 minutes.

Whisk the flour into the strained drippings in a saucepan. Cook over medium heat for 3 minutes, stirring constantly. Add the broth and water gradually, whisking constantly. Bring to a boil. Stir in the vinegar and salt to taste. Cook until thickened to desired consistency, stirring constantly.

Discard the strings from the roast and cut into ½-inch slices. Arrange the slices on a warm platter; garnish with rosemary sprigs. Serve with the gravy.

MARINATED PORK TENDERLOIN

Serves 4 to 6

Cook this on the grill for easy entertaining. The jalapeño pepper and pepper flakes give it a zippy flavor.

1	jalapeño pepper, minced
1	(1-inch) piece of ginger, minced
⅓	cup honey
3	tablespoons sesame oil
3	tablespoons soy sauce
¼	teaspoon crushed red pepper flakes
2	(1-pound) pork tenderloins

Wine Suggestion
California
Chardonnay

Combine the jalapeño pepper, ginger, honey, sesame oil, soy sauce and red pepper flakes in a plastic food storage bag. Add the pork tenderloins. Marinate in the refrigerator overnight; drain. Grill over medium-hot coals for 20 minutes or until cooked through; do not overcook. Cut lengthwise into thin slices.

BARBECUED COUNTRY PORK RIBS

Serves 4

Serve these ribs with a baked potato and braised fresh spinach. The barbecue sauce can also be used to prepare chicken.

8	country pork ribs
1	cup packed dark brown sugar
3	tablespoons white vinegar
1	cup barbecue sauce, must not be hickory smoked
1/2	cup (or less) catsup
	Worcestershire sauce to taste
1	teaspoon prepared mustard
1/4	teaspoon garlic salt
1/4	teaspoon onion salt

Wine Suggestion
Zinfandel

Trim the ribs and arrange in a baking dish. Bake at 350 degrees for 15 minutes.

Blend the brown sugar and vinegar in a saucepan. Add the barbecue sauce, catsup, Worcestershire sauce, mustard, garlic salt and onion salt; mix well. Simmer for 10 minutes, stirring occasionally.

Drain the ribs. Pour the sauce over the top. Bake for 45 to 60 minutes longer or until cooked through.

OVEN-BARBECUED SPARERIBS

Serves 4 to 6

Enjoy the flavor of barbecue any time of the year with this oven-barbecue recipe. Serve the ribs with corn bread.

4	pounds pork spareribs
	Salt to taste
1	clove of garlic, minced
1	tablespoon butter
1/2	cup catsup
1/3	cup chili sauce
2	tablespoons brown sugar
2	tablespoons chopped onion
1	tablespoon mustard
1	tablespoon Worcestershire sauce
	Hot pepper sauce to taste
3	thin lemon slices
1	teaspoon celery seeds
1/4	teaspoon salt

Wine Suggestions
Beer or California
Zinfandel

Cut the ribs into serving pieces. Combine with salt to taste and water to cover in saucepan. Simmer, covered, for 1 hour or until nearly tender.

Sauté the garlic in the butter in a saucepan for 4 to 5 minutes or until tender. Add the catsup, chili sauce, brown sugar, onion, mustard, Worcestershire sauce, pepper sauce, lemon slices, celery seeds and 1/4 teaspoon salt; mix well.

Drain the ribs and place in a shallow baking pan. Pour the barbecue sauce over the top. Bake at 350 degrees for 20 minutes or until cooked through, basting frequently.

PAELLA

Serves 6 to 8

Paella, a wonderful one-dish meal, is a traditional dish of Spain.

2   chicken breast filets
12   ounces veal tip steak
1   pound center-cut pork loin
2   green bell peppers
1/2 cup olive oil
4   ounces fresh mushrooms, thinly sliced
1/2 cup olive oil
1   large clove of garlic, minced
1   large onion, minced
2   cups uncooked long grain rice
1/4 teaspoon saffron
1/2 teaspoon oregano
4   (to 5) cups chicken broth
8   ounces bay scallops
1   pound uncooked shrimp
1   (4-ounce) jar chopped pimentos
     Salt to taste
1   (10-ounce) package frozen peas or 1 pound fresh peas
     Pepper to taste

Wine Suggestion
Medium-bodied
Spanish Red Wine

Cut the chicken and veal into 1-inch pieces. Rinse the chicken and pat dry. Trim the pork loin and slice it 1/4 inch thick; cut the slices into 1-inch pieces. Cut the green peppers into 1/2-inch pieces. Sauté the pork in 1/2 cup heated olive oil in a large skillet until deep brown; remove with a slotted spoon and drain. Sauté the chicken and veal until light brown; remove with a slotted spoon and drain. Sauté the green peppers and mushrooms just until tender, adding additional oil if needed; remove with a slotted spoon and drain.

Wash and dry the skillet. Heat 1/2 cup olive oil in the skillet over low heat. Add the garlic, onion, rice, saffron and oregano. Sauté for 5 minutes, stirring constantly. Return the pork, chicken and veal to the skillet. Add the chicken broth, scallops, shrimp, green pepper mixture and pimentos. Add 1 to 2 teaspoons salt if the chicken broth is unsalted. Bring to a boil; reduce the heat. Simmer, covered, for 20 minutes. Add the peas. Simmer, covered, for 20 minutes longer, stirring gently occasionally. Season with salt and pepper to taste. You may use saffron-flavored rice if you prefer.

HAM BRAISED IN MADEIRA

Serves 12 to 16

The ham makes a beautiful presentation on a buffet table for a dinner party. Raisins and mushrooms may be added to the sauce.

The ham

1   cup each sliced carrots, onion and celery
2   tablespoons each butter and vegetable oil
1   (14-pound) bone-in fully cooked ham, trimmed
2   cups Madeira
3   cups beef stock or bouillon
6   sprigs of parsley
1/2 teaspoon thyme
1   bay leaf

The sauce

3   tablespoons arrowroot
2   tablespoons wine or stock
3   tablespoons butter

Wine Suggestions
French Tavel or Dry
California Rosé

Sauté the carrots, onion and celery in the butter and oil in a baking pan until light brown. Place the ham on the vegetables in the pan. Add the wine, beef stock, parsley, thyme and bay leaf. Bake at 325 degrees for 2 to 2½ hours or until ham is tender, basting every 20 minutes. Remove the ham to a serving platter.

Strain the cooking juices into a saucepan; skim off the fat. Cook until reduced to about 3 cups. Blend the arrowroot with the wine in a cup. Stir into the saucepan. Cook for 5 minutes or until thickened, stirring constantly. Whisk in the butter. Serve with the ham.

INDONESIAN SATE

Serves 6

Grilled skewers of pork, chicken and beef make great picnic appetizers. You may prepare them in advance and freeze them until needed.

1   cup salted peanuts
1½ cups chopped onions
2   cloves of garlic, minced
2   tablespoons brown sugar
3   tablespoons lemon juice
5   tablespoons soy sauce
2   tablespoons ground coriander
1   teaspoon crushed red pepper
1/2 teaspoon black pepper
1/2 cup melted butter
1/2 cup chicken stock
2   pounds chicken, lean pork and beef

Wine Suggestion
California
Gewurztraminer

Combine the peanuts, onions, garlic, brown sugar, lemon juice, soy sauce, coriander, red pepper and black pepper in a food processor or blender container. Process until smooth. Spoon the mixture into a saucepan. Bring to a boil; pour into shallow dish. Stir in the butter and chicken stock. Cool to room temperature. Rinse the chicken and pat dry. Cut the chicken, pork and beef into strips. Add to the marinade. Marinate for 1 to 2 hours. Drain, reserving the marinade. Thread the meat onto skewers. Grill until cooked through, basting occasionally.

PERFECT ROAST LEG OF LAMB

Serves 6 to 8

Serve this with fresh asparagus and parslied new potatoes for an elegant Easter dinner. It is also good with the Stuffed Peppers on page 115.

The sauce

1	(6-ounce) can frozen orange juice concentrate, thawed
1/4	cup dry red wine
1/4	cup butter

The lamb

1	(6-pound) leg of lamb
2	cloves of garlic, minced
1	tablespoon paprika
1	tablespoon fresh rosemary or 1½ teaspoons dried rosemary
2	teaspoons salt
1/2	teaspoon pepper

Combine the orange juice concentrate, wine and butter in a saucepan. Simmer for 15 minutes.

Make 12 slits in the lamb with the point of a knife. Combine the garlic, paprika, rosemary, salt and pepper in a small bowl; mix well. Press the seasoning mixture into the slits. Insert a meat thermometer into the thickest part of the lamb, taking care not to touch the bone. Place in a roasting pan. Roast for 12 to 15 minutes per pound or to 130 to 135 degrees for rare, for 20 minutes per pound or to 140 degrees for medium, or for 30 to 35 minutes per pound or to 160 degrees for well done, basting frequently with some of the orange sauce after the first hour of roasting time. Remove the lamb to a warm platter. Let stand for 15 minutes before carving.

Pour the pan juices into the remaining orange sauce. Let stand for 15 minutes; pour off the fat. Serve with the lamb.

MEDITERRANEAN LAMB CHOPS

Serves 2 or 3

Serve with Greek salad and roasted potatoes for great summer entertaining.

4	cloves of garlic, crushed
1	tablespoon olive oil
1	tablespoon oregano
1	teaspoon rosemary
1	teaspoon salt
1	pound lamb chops

Wine Suggestions
Greek Rodytis or
Italian Brunella

Combine the garlic, olive oil, oregano, rosemary and salt in a bowl; mix into a paste. Rub the paste over both sides of the lamb chops. Marinate, covered, in the refrigerator for up to 12 hours. Grill until done to taste.

LAMB STEW OVER RICE

Serves 5 or 6

Serve this Lebanese dish with a salad and Lebanese or pita bread for a delicious dinner any time of the year.

The stew

2	pounds lamb shoulder, cut into 1-inch cubes
1	medium onion, sliced lengthwise
2	cloves of garlic, minced
1	(16-ounce) can whole tomatoes, crushed
1	(12-ounce) can tomato paste
1	(12-ounce) can water
1/4	teaspoon cinnamon
1	teaspoon salt
1/2	teaspoon pepper
2	cups fresh pea pods

The rice

1/3	cup broken vermicelli or angel hair pasta
1/4	cup butter or margarine
1	cup uncooked long grain rice
2 1/2	cups water
3/4	(to 1) teaspoon salt

Wine Suggestion
Greek Rodytis

Cook the lamb in its own juices in a large skillet over medium heat until the pink color disappears. Add the onion and garlic. Cook, covered, until the onion is tender, the lamb is brown and the juices have evaporated. Combine with the tomatoes, tomato paste, water, cinnamon, salt and pepper in a 4-quart saucepan. Stir additional water into skillet to deglaze and add to saucepan. Simmer for 1 hour, stirring occasionally. Add pea pods. Simmer for 5 minutes longer.

Sauté the vermicelli in the butter in a 3-quart saucepan until dark golden brown. Add the rice; mix well. Sauté for 30 seconds. Stir in water and salt. Simmer, covered, until liquid is absorbed and rice is tender; do not stir. Serve the stew over the rice.

ALMOND LEMON CHICKEN

Serves 6

This is quick and easy to prepare with a very special flavor.

6   chicken breast filets
5   tablespoons lemon juice
3   tablespoons Dijon mustard
2   cloves of garlic, finely chopped
1/4 teaspoon white pepper
5   tablespoons olive oil
1   cup sliced almonds
1 1/2 tablespoons olive oil
2   cups chicken broth
1   teaspoon cornstarch
1   tablespoon water
2   tablespoons lemon or orange marmalade
2   tablespoons butter, cut into pieces
2   tablespoons chopped fresh parsley
     Red pepper flakes to taste

Wine Suggestion
California
Chardonnay

Rinse the chicken and pat dry. Pour mixture of lemon juice, Dijon mustard, garlic, white pepper and 5 tablespoons olive oil over the chicken in a shallow dish, tossing to coat. Marinate at room temperature for 1 hour, turning occasionally. Sauté the almonds in 1 1/2 teaspoons of the olive oil in a skillet until brown. Remove to a bowl; wipe the skillet. Drain the chicken, reserving the marinade. Cook the chicken in the remaining 1 1/2 teaspoons olive oil in the skillet over high heat for 6 to 10 minutes or until brown on both sides. Remove the chicken to a platter. Strain the marinade. Add the marinade to the skillet. Stir in a mixture of broth, cornstarch and water. Cook over high heat for 5 minutes or until the mixture is reduced by half, stirring occasionally. Stir in the marmalade. Cook over medium heat until blended, stirring constantly. Add the butter, parsley, red pepper flakes and chicken; mix well. Cook over high heat until heated through, stirring occasionally. Stir in the almonds. Garnish with lemon slices.

GINGER CHICKEN

Serves 4 to 6

Serve hot or cold as an appetizer or with brown rice as a main dish.

The sauce

1 cup soy sauce
1 cup sugar
2 tablespoons ground ginger

The chicken

8 chicken breast filets
1 cup flour
1 cup bread crumbs
2 teaspoons paprika
1 teaspoon salt
Garlic powder to taste
3 eggs, beaten
Vegetable oil for frying

Wine Suggestions
White Rhone-style
wine or Pinot Blanc

Combine the soy sauce, sugar and ginger in a saucepan; mix well. Simmer until the sugar dissolves, stirring frequently.

Rinse the chicken and pat dry. Cut into bite-sized pieces or larger strips. Combine the flour, bread crumbs, paprika, salt and garlic powder in a bowl; mix well. Dip the chicken in the flour mixture, the eggs and again into the flour mixture. Fry in hot oil in a skillet until brown on both sides, turning once; drain. Dip the chicken into the soy sauce mixture, tossing to coat. Place on baking sheet in 200-degree oven to keep warm.

LEMON-BASIL GRILLED CHICKEN

Serves 6

Light, low-fat and easy to prepare.

8 chicken breast filets
1/2 cup vegetable oil
1/4 cup lemon juice
2 tablespoons white wine vinegar
2 cloves of garlic, crushed
1/2 teaspoon salt
1/4 teaspoon pepper
1/2 cup chopped fresh basil
1 teaspoon dried basil

Wine Suggestion
Chardonnay

Rinse the chicken and pat dry. Arrange in a nonmetallic dish. Pour mixture of oil, lemon juice, wine vinegar, garlic, salt, pepper, fresh basil and dried basil over the chicken, tossing to coat. Marinate, covered, in the refrigerator for 2 hours, turning occasionally; drain. Grill over medium-hot coals for 10 to 15 minutes or until the chicken is tender.

GRILLED TERIYAKI CHICKEN

Serves 4 to 6

Great for busy nights during soccer and baseball seasons.

1½ (to 2) pounds chicken pieces, skinned
½ cup soy sauce
¼ cup dry sherry
2 tablespoons sugar
2 tablespoons grated ginger
4 cloves of garlic, crushed
2 tablespoons vegetable oil

Wine Suggestion
White Rhone wine
such as Marsanne

Rinse the chicken and pat dry. Arrange in a nonmetallic dish. Pour mixture of soy sauce, sherry, sugar, ginger, garlic and oil over chicken, tossing to coat. Marinate, covered, in the refrigerator for 6 hours or longer, turning occasionally; drain. Grill over hot coals for 30 minutes or until the chicken is tender. Serve hot or cold.

JAMBALAYA

Serves 8 to 10

Intensify the flavor by adding additional hot sauce and red pepper flakes.

2 whole chicken breasts, skinned, boned
Chicken stock
1 pound Italian sausage
2 onions, chopped
1 red bell pepper, chopped
1 green bell pepper, chopped
1 clove of garlic, minced
3 (to 4) tablespoons vegetable oil
3 cups canned plum tomatoes
1 cup tomato juice
½ teaspoon each thyme and pepper
1 teaspoon hot sauce
½ teaspoon red pepper flakes
1 teaspoon Tabasco sauce
1½ cups chicken broth
1 cup uncooked rice
1 pound shrimp, peeled, deveined
½ cup chopped scallions
¼ cup chopped fresh parsley

Wine Suggestion
French Beaujolais

Rinse the chicken. Pound the chicken between sheets of waxed paper to flatten. Combine the chicken with enough chicken stock to cover in a baking pan. Poach in a 350-degree oven for 20 minutes; drain. Chop the chicken. Brown the sausage in a skillet, stirring until crumbly; drain. Sauté the onions, red pepper, green pepper and garlic in oil in a stockpot until vegetables are tender. Stir in the tomatoes and tomato juice. Add the chicken, sausage, thyme, pepper, hot sauce, red pepper flakes, Tabasco sauce, broth and rice; mix well. Bring to a boil; reduce heat. Simmer, covered for 30 minutes, stirring occasionally. Stir in the shrimp, scallions and parsley. Cook for 5 minutes or until the shrimp turn pink. May add additional liquid if needed for desired consistency. Serve with crusty French bread.

MONTEREY CHICKEN

Serves 6

Serve with a salad, vegetable and crusty French bread.

8	chicken breast filets
6	ounces Monterey Jack cheese, cut into 8 strips
2	eggs, beaten
3/4	cup seasoned bread crumbs
1/4	cup margarine
1/2	cup chopped onion
2	tablespoons flour
1	teaspoon salt
1/2	teaspoon pepper
1	cup chicken stock
3	ounces mushrooms, sliced
3	cups cooked rice

Wine Suggestion
Sauvignon Blanc

Rinse the chicken and pat dry. Pound the chicken between sheets of waxed paper to flatten. Place 1 piece of cheese on each filet. Roll to enclose cheese; secure with wooden pick. Dip in the eggs in a bowl; coat with the bread crumbs. Sauté the chicken rolls in the margarine in a skillet until brown on all sides. Remove to a platter. Sauté the onion in the same skillet until tender, adding additional margarine if needed. Stir in the flour, salt, pepper and chicken stock. Cook until thickened, stirring constantly. Add the mushrooms and cooked rice; mix well. Spoon into a greased shallow baking dish; top with the chicken rolls. Bake, covered, at 400 degrees for 30 minutes.

CHICKEN PICCATA

Serves 2

This low-fat dish is shared by Chef Bryan Carstens of the Mauh Nah Tee See Country Club. Serve it with wild rice and glazed carrots.

2	whole chicken breasts, boned, skinned
1/2	cup flour
1	tablespoon canola oil
1	teaspoon chopped shallots
1	tablespoon capers
1/2	cup white wine
1 1/2	cups chicken stock
	Juice of 1 lemon
1	tablespoon cornstarch
1	tablespoon water
	Salt and pepper to taste

Wine Suggestion
Pinot Grigio

Rinse the chicken and pat dry. Fold each chicken breast in half; coat with flour. Sauté in the canola oil in a skillet until brown on both sides. Place in a baking dish. Bake at 350 degrees for 20 minutes. Sauté the shallots and capers in the pan drippings until the shallots are light brown. Stir in the white wine. Cook until the wine is reduced by 1/2, stirring constantly. Add the stock and lemon juice. Simmer for 1 minute, stirring constantly. Stir in a mixture of cornstarch and water. Cook until of desired consistency, stirring constantly. Simmer for 1 minute, stirring constantly. Season with salt and pepper. Spoon over the chicken. Garnish with lemon slices and chopped fresh parsley.

ROQUEFORT AND LEMON CHICKEN

Serves 6

Bleu cheese is also good in this recipe. Garnish with chopped parsley and grated lemon rind.

6	chicken breasts
1/4	cup flour
1	teaspoon salt
1	teaspoon rosemary, crushed
1/4	teaspoon pepper
3	tablespoons butter
2/3	cup sour cream
1/2	cup crumbled Roquefort cheese
2	tablespoons fresh lemon juice
1	tablespoon sliced green onions
2	teaspoons grated lemon rind

Wine Suggestion
Merlot

Rinse the chicken and pat dry. Coat with a mixture of flour, salt, rosemary and pepper. Brown the chicken in the butter in a skillet over medium-high heat for 5 minutes, turning once. Arrange the chicken skin side up in a baking dish. Spread with a mixture of sour cream, cheese, lemon juice, green onions and lemon rind. Bake at 350 degrees for 30 minutes or until the chicken is tender and the topping is brown.

RATATOUILLE WITH CHICKEN AND PESTO

Serves 6

The smell while this is cooking is almost as wonderful as the taste.

2	whole chicken breasts, boned, skinned
1	medium red onion, thinly sliced
1	medium green bell pepper, chopped
4	cloves of garlic, crushed
1/4	cup olive oil
1	small eggplant, chopped
	Salt and black pepper to taste
2	small zucchini, cut into bite-sized pieces
3	tablespoons chopped fresh basil or 1 tablespoon dried basil
2	teaspoons oregano
1	teaspoon thyme
4	medium tomatoes, peeled, seeded, chopped
8	ounces mushrooms, sliced
1	(8-ounce) can tomato sauce
	Cayenne pepper to taste
1/2	cup orzo, cooked, drained

Rinse the chicken and pat dry. Cut into thin slices. Sauté the red onion, green pepper and garlic in the olive oil in a skillet for 2 minutes. Stir in the eggplant. Sauté for several minutes. Season with salt and black pepper. Stir in the zucchini. Sauté for 2 minutes. Add the chicken, basil, oregano, thyme and additional black pepper; mix well. Cook over high heat until the chicken is tender, stirring constantly. Stir in the tomatoes, mushrooms, tomato sauce and cayenne pepper. Adjust the seasonings. Simmer, covered, until of desired consistency. Stir in the orzo. May be prepared in advance, chilled until serving time and reheated on the stove or in the oven.

SESAME AND GINGER CHICKEN

Serves 4

A slightly different addition to your chicken repertory—it is low-fat, quick and easy. It can be broiled as well as grilled.

4   chicken breast filets
1   tablespoon sesame seeds
2   tablespoons honey
2   tablespoons low-sodium soy sauce
2   teaspoons grated fresh ginger

Wine Suggestion
Gewurztraminer

Rinse the chicken and pat dry. Pound 1/4 inch thick between 2 sheets of heavy-duty plastic wrap. Place the sesame seeds on a small baking sheet. Toast in a 375-degree oven for 7 minutes, stirring occasionally. Spray grill rack with nonstick cooking spray. Grill chicken over hot coals for 4 minutes per side, basting frequently with mixture of sesame seeds, honey, soy sauce and ginger. Garnish with green onions.

SPICY THAI-STYLE CHICKEN AND RICE

Serves 6

Enjoy the popularity of Thai cooking with this dish, which has just the right amount of zip.

6   (5-ounce) chicken breast filets
1/4   cup soy sauce
1   cup uncooked rice
1   clove of garlic, minced
2   teaspoons vegetable oil
2 1/4 cups chicken broth
2   tablespoons creamy peanut butter
1/2   teaspoon red pepper flakes or 1/4 teaspoon cayenne pepper
1 1/2 cups pea pods
1   tablespoon finely shredded fresh ginger
1   small red bell pepper, cut into strips
2   tablespoons peanut halves

Wine Suggestions
French Graves or
White Beaujolais

Rinse the chicken and pat dry. Combine the chicken and soy sauce in a bowl, tossing to coat. Let stand at room temperature. Sauté the rice and garlic in the oil in a skillet for 1 minute. Stir in the broth, peanut butter and red pepper flakes. Bring to a boil. Boil until peanut butter melts, stirring constantly. Drain the chicken, reserving the soy sauce. Arrange the chicken over the rice mixture; pour the soy sauce over the chicken. Simmer, covered, for 40 minutes or until the chicken is tender. Stir in the pea pods and ginger; sprinkle with the red pepper strips. Remove from the heat. Let stand, covered, for 5 minutes or until the liquid has been absorbed. Sprinkle with the peanuts.

TARRAGON CHICKEN BREASTS

Serves 6

Fresh tarragon gives this dish its unique flavor. Use dried tarragon if fresh is not available.

6   chicken breast filets
3   tablespoons butter
2   tablespoons olive oil
2   shallots, chopped
1/2 cup each white wine and chicken stock
1   large clove of garlic, minced
3/4 cup half and half
1   tablespoon Dijon mustard
1   tablespoon chopped fresh tarragon or 1 teaspoon dried tarragon
1/2 teaspoon thyme
     Pepper to taste

Rinse the chicken and pat dry. Sauté the chicken in 2 tablespoons of the butter and 1 tablespoon of the olive oil in a skillet until brown on both sides, turning once. Remove to a warm platter; cover with foil. Stir the remaining butter and olive oil into the pan drippings. Cook until foamy. Stir in the shallots. Sauté for 2 minutes. Add the wine, stock and garlic. Bring to a boil. Boil until the mixture is reduced to 1/2 cup, stirring frequently. Whisk in the half and half and mustard. Boil until thickened, stirring constantly. Add the tarragon, thyme and pepper. Return the chicken to the skillet; mix well. Cook for 5 minutes or until heated through. Garnish with parsley sprigs.

CHICKEN VESUVIO AND POTATOES

Serves 6 to 8

Great Italian flavor! The peas add color.

1   (3-pound) chicken, cut up
     Salt and pepper to taste
     Oregano to taste
     Vegetable oil for frying
1   clove of garlic, crushed
1/2 cup red wine
1/2 cup water
1   clove of garlic, crushed
1   cup green peas, cooked, drained
     Red potatoes, cut into 1x3-inch pieces
     Garlic powder to taste
1   clove of garlic, crushed

Wine Suggestion
Bardolino

Rinse the chicken and pat dry. Sprinkle with the salt, pepper and oregano. Fry the chicken in oil with 1 clove of garlic in a skillet until brown on both sides, turning once. Discard the garlic. Drain, reserving the pan drippings. Add the chicken, wine, water and 1 clove of garlic to skillet. Simmer, covered, for 30 minutes, stirring occasionally. Stir in the peas at the end of the cooking cycle. Sprinkle the potatoes with the garlic powder and oregano. Strain reserved pan drippings into skillet. Add 1 clove of garlic and potatoes. Fry for 20 minutes or until brown on all sides; drain. Arrange the chicken on a serving platter; spoon the sauce over the chicken. Serve with the fried potatoes.

ROCK CORNISH HENS

Serves 4

This recipe can also be prepared with pheasant.

4   Rock Cornish game hens
    Salt and pepper to taste
2   tablespoons melted butter
3/4 cup orange juice
1/2 cup Madeira
1/2 cup packed brown sugar
2   tablespoons lemon juice
1   teaspoon dry mustard
1/2 teaspoon allspice
1/4 teaspoon salt

Wine Suggestions
Pinot Noir or
Zinfandel

Rinse the Cornish hens and pat dry. Sprinkle with the salt and pepper. Place in a baking pan; drizzle with the melted butter. Bake at 325 degrees for 30 minutes. Combine the orange juice, Madeira, brown sugar, lemon juice, dry mustard, allspice and salt in a saucepan; mix well. Simmer for 5 minutes, stirring occasionally. Baste the Cornish hens with the orange juice mixture. Bake for 30 to 45 minutes or until the Cornish hens are tender.

CORNISH HENS

Serves 2 to 4

This is a good dish to serve with wild rice in the fall.

The Cornish hens

    Butter, softened
    Bacon slices
    Salt and pepper to taste
2   Cornish game hens, split
12 (to 16) dried juniper berries
1   (to 2) ounces gin

The sauce

1   (8-ounce) jar red currant jelly
    Juice of 2 oranges
1   teaspoon prepared mustard
    Salt to taste
    Cayenne pepper to taste

Wine Suggestion
Unfiltered
California Zinfandel

Rub a metal baking pan with butter; do not use glass. Line with the bacon; sprinkle generously with the salt and pepper. Rinse the Cornish hens and pat dry. Rub with the butter; sprinkle with the salt and pepper. Place skin side up in the prepared pan. Tuck 3 to 4 juniper berries under each half. Bake at 500 degrees for 15 minutes. Pour mixture of gin and a small amount of warm water over the Cornish hens. Reduce the temperature to 350 degrees. Bake for 45 minutes, basting frequently.

Combine the jelly, orange juice, mustard, salt and cayenne pepper in a saucepan; mix well. Cook over medium-low heat until blended, stirring occasionally. Serve warm with the hens.

TURKEY WITH RAISINS AND CAPERS

Serves 6 to 8

Great to serve company because it can be prepared in advance.

1	(5½- to 6-pound) turkey breast
1	large onion, chopped
3	carrots, chopped
2	bay leaves
1	teaspoon whole black peppercorns
6	tablespoons white vinegar
	Salt to taste
2/3	cup golden raisins
6	tablespoons fresh lemon juice
1	tablespoon balsamic vinegar
1	cup olive oil
	Pepper to taste
	Zest of 2 large lemons
1/4	cup capers
2	tablespoons finely chopped fresh parsley
2	tablespoons finely shredded fresh mint
6	tablespoons pine nuts or chopped walnuts, toasted

Wine Suggestion
Sauvignon Blanc

Place the turkey breast in a stockpot. Add enough cold water to measure 1 inch above the turkey breast; remove the turkey breast to a platter. Add the onion, carrots, bay leaves, peppercorns and white vinegar; mix well. Bring to a boil. Stir in the salt. Return the turkey breast to the stockpot; reduce the heat. Simmer, covered, for 30 minutes; drain. Place in a dish just large enough to hold. Soak the raisins in boiling water in a covered bowl for 5 minutes; drain. Whisk the lemon juice, balsamic vinegar, olive oil, salt and pepper in a bowl until blended. Stir in the lemon zest, raisins and capers. Pour over the turkey. Marinate, covered, in the refrigerator for 4 hours to overnight, stirring once. Let stand at room temperature for 20 minutes. Drain, reserving the marinade. Slice the turkey into 1/4-inch diagonal slices; arrange on a platter. Stir the parsley and mint into the reserved marinade. Spoon over the turkey. Sprinkle with the pine nuts.

DUCK BREAST WITH PORT SAUCE

Serves 8

This was enjoyed in an 18th century manor house in France. It is an excellent dish for a special dinner or celebration. For a classic presentation, nap the plates with puréed parsnips, arrange the sliced duck in the center and spoon the sauce around the edge.

The marinade

1½ cups dry red wine
½ cup balsamic vinegar
3 tablespoons soy sauce
½ cup fresh lemon juice
4 cloves of garlic, minced
½ cup olive oil
1½ tablespoons grated fresh ginger
Salt and pepper to taste

The duck

2 (2-pound) boneless duck breasts with skin
Salt and pepper to taste

The sauce

3 tablespoons sugar
3 tablespoons water
2 tablespoons white wine vinegar
3 tablespoons balsamic vinegar
¼ cup minced shallot
1 large clove of garlic, minced
2 tablespoons butter or duck fat
1¾ cups dry red wine
¾ cup beef broth
½ cup whipping cream
½ cup tawny port
3 tablespoons flour
¼ cup unsalted butter, softened

Wine Suggestions
French Burgundy or
California Pinot Noir

Combine the wine, vinegar, soy sauce, lemon juice, garlic, olive oil, ginger, salt and pepper in a sealable plastic food storage bag.

Add the duck, mixing to coat well. Marinate in the refrigerator overnight. Drain the duck and pat dry. Score the skin in a crisscross pattern at 1-inch intervals, taking care not to cut through the fat to the meat; sprinkle with salt and pepper. Heat 2 ovenproof skillets over medium-high heat. Add 1 duck breast skin side down to each skillet. Cook for 10 minutes. Turn duck and cook for 2 minutes longer. Roast at 450 degrees for 5 to 7 minutes or until done to taste. Slice diagonally cross grain into thin slices; arrange on warm serving plates.

Bring the sugar and water to a boil in a heavy saucepan, stirring to dissolve the sugar. Boil until the mixture is a caramel color. Stir in the vinegars gradually. Sauté the shallot and garlic in 2 tablespoons butter in a skillet over medium heat until tender. Add the dry red wine. Boil until the mixture is reduced by ½. Add the beef broth. Boil until the mixture is reduced by ⅓. Press the mixture through a fine sieve into the vinegar mixture. The sauce may be prepared to this point in advance and finished at serving time. Whisk in the cream and port wine. Simmer for 1 minute. Blend the flour and ¼ cup butter in a small bowl. Add to the sauce. Cook until thickened, stirring constantly. Stir in any juices which have accumulated from the duck. Serve the sauce with the duck.

FISH STEW PROVENCALE

Serves 16

To use the leftover broth, go out and restock the pond!

The croutons

1	loaf French bread
	Garlic cloves, sliced into halves
	Olive oil

The stew base

2	ounces flat anchovies, chopped
1/4	cup chopped parsley
4	teaspoons minced garlic
1/4	teaspoon cayenne pepper
1	cup olive oil
3	cups dry red wine
1	(28-ounce) can crushed tomatoes

The stew

8	fresh clams in the shells
4	fresh oysters in the shells
1	pound cod, cut into large pieces
1	pound halibut, cut into large pieces
1	pound turbot, cut into large pieces
1	pound large scallions, sliced

Wine Suggestion
French Puilly Fuisse

Slice the French bread 1/2 inch thick; arrange on a baking sheet. Toast at 450 degrees until golden brown. Rub with the fresh garlic and brush with a small amount of olive oil.

Sauté the anchovies, parsley and garlic with the cayenne pepper in the olive oil in a large saucepan over medium heat until golden brown, stirring frequently. Add the wine and tomatoes; reduce the heat. Simmer for 3 hours or until reduced to a very thick base.

Heat the clams and oysters in their shells in a skillet until the shells open. Remove the clams and oysters from their shells, discarding the shells; strain and reserve the juices. Add the fish, clams, oysters and reserved juices to the base. Add scallions and enough water to cover. Simmer for 15 minutes or until the fish flakes easily; mixture does not need to boil. Place 1 crouton in each bowl. Spoon soup over croutons.

ORANGE ROUGHY WITH MUSHROOM SAUCE

Serves 4

Not all creamy sauces have to be laden with cholesterol. Use yogurt at room temperature in this recipe for a very creamy and smooth-textured sauce.

1½   cups sliced mushrooms
¾   cup chopped onion
⅛   teaspoon pepper
1   cup plain low-fat yogurt, at room temperature
¼   cup grated Parmesan cheese
4   (4-ounce) orange roughy filets or other lean white fish
2   tablespoons fine dry bread crumbs

Wine Suggestion
California
Chardonnay

Spray a large nonstick skillet with cooking spray. Heat over medium heat. Add the mushrooms, onion and pepper. Sauté for 3 minutes. Cool. Combine with the yogurt and cheese in a bowl; mix well.

Place the fish in a 7x11-inch baking dish. Top with the mushroom mixture and bread crumbs. Bake at 350 degrees for 30 minutes or until the fish flakes easily. Garnish with paprika and parsley sprigs.

RED SNAPPER A L'ORANGE

Serves 6

This easy recipe is based on the guidelines of the American Heart Association.

1½   pounds red snapper filets
2   tablespoons orange juice
1   teaspoon grated orange rind
3   tablespoons vegetable oil
       Nutmeg and freshly ground pepper to taste

Wine Suggestion
Sauvignon Blanc

Cut the fish into 6 serving pieces. Arrange in a single layer in an oiled baking pan. Combine the orange juice, orange rind, oil, nutmeg and pepper in a small bowl; mix well. Pour over the fish. Bake at 350 degrees for 20 to 30 minutes or until the fish flakes easily.

GRILLED SALMON

Serves 6

There is no cleanup with this easy recipe for the grill.

2   tablespoons lemon juice
2   tablespoons olive oil
2   tablespoons butter
1   tablespoon Dijon mustard
1   tablespoon garlic powder
1   teaspoon basil
1   teaspoon dill
1   teaspoon white pepper
     Salt to taste
3   pounds fresh salmon filets

Wine Suggestions
Oregon or
Washington
State Chardonnay

Combine the lemon juice, olive oil, butter, mustard, garlic powder, basil, dill, white pepper and salt in a small saucepan. Bring to a boil; reduce the heat. Simmer for 10 minutes.

Make a pan large enough to hold the salmon from heavy-duty foil. Place the salmon skin side down in the pan. Pour the heated sauce over the fish; top with foil. Grill for 10 minutes or until the fish flakes easily.

SALMON STEAKS WITH DILL AND CAPERS

Serves 6

Even salmon skeptics enjoyed this moist and flavorful dish.

6   salmon steaks
1   tablespoon fresh lemon juice
1/2   teaspoon marjoram
1/2   teaspoon garlic powder
1/2   teaspoon salt
1/4   teaspoon pepper
1/4   cup melted butter
1   cup sliced green onions
       Fresh dill and drained capers to taste

Wine Suggestions
Oegon or
Washington State
Chardonnay

Place the salmon in a shallow baking dish. Sprinkle with the lemon juice, marjoram, garlic powder, salt and pepper; drizzle with butter. Top with the green onions, dill and capers. Bake at 350 degrees for 15 minutes. Remove and discard the skin from the steaks. Bake for 5 minutes longer or until the fish flakes easily.

HERBED SHRIMP DE JONGHE

Serves 4

Great taste! Serve over rice or fettucini with crisp French bread.

1/2	cup butter, softened
3	cloves of garlic, crushed
2	teaspoons chopped chives
1	teaspoon tarragon
2	teaspoons chopped parsley
	Mace, thyme, nutmeg, salt, black pepper and cayenne pepper to taste
2	tablespoons sherry
1/4	cup (about) fresh bread crumbs
12	ounces fresh shrimp, peeled, deveined

Wine Suggestions
White Rhine-style
wine such as
Viogniere or
Marsanne

Combine the butter with the garlic, chives, tarragon, parsley, mace, thyme, nutmeg, salt, black pepper and cayenne pepper in a bowl. Add the wine; mix well. Add enough bread crumbs to form a paste-like mixture. Chill for 2 hours or longer.

Let butter mixture stand at room temperature for 1 hour. Cut the shrimp into halves lengthwise. Place in a shallow baking dish. Spread the herbed butter evenly over the shrimp. Bake at 400 degrees for 15 minutes.

MUSTARD BROILED SHRIMP

Serves 4

Serve this over rice for a low-calorie main dish or with wooden picks for an appetizer. You may use commercially-prepared honey mustard or mix honey with grainy mustard for a sweet-hot taste.

3	tablespoons honey mustard
2	tablespoons dark soy sauce
1/4	teaspoon Tabasco sauce
1	pound large shrimp, peeled

Wine Suggestion
Sauvignon Blanc

Combine the honey mustard, soy sauce and Tabasco sauce in a bowl. Add the shrimp, stirring to coat well. Remove the shrimp from the sauce, reserving the sauce. Arrange the shrimp in a single layer on a baking sheet lined with foil. Broil about 5 inches from the heat source for 2 minutes on each side, turning with tongs. Bring the reserved mustard sauce to a boil in a small saucepan. Cook for 1 to 2 minutes. Serve with the shrimp.

RISOTTO WITH SHRIMP

Serves 4

Arborio rice gives this dish its distinct flavor. It is frequently used in northern Italy.

1	medium onion, thinly sliced
2	tablespoons butter
1	pound uncooked shrimp, peeled, deveined
1/2	cup dry white wine
1 1/2	cups uncooked arborio rice
2	cups chicken broth
1	cup water
1/4	cup grated Parmesan cheese
	Pepper to taste

Wine Suggestion
Italian Pinot Grigio

Sauté the onion in the butter in a 12-inch skillet over medium-high heat. Reduce the heat to medium and add the shrimp. Cook for 8 minutes, turning once. Remove the shrimp to a warm dish with a slotted spoon. Add the wine to the skillet, stirring to deglaze. Cook for 5 minutes. Add the rice. Cook over medium heat for 5 minutes or until the rice is light brown. Mix the chicken broth and water in a bowl. Add half the mixture to the rice. Cook until the liquid is absorbed. Add the remaining broth mixture. Cook until absorbed. Stir in the shrimp. Cook just until heated through. Sprinkle with the cheese and pepper.

SPICY BAKED SHRIMP

Serves 4

Serve with fresh French bread for soaking up the sauce, which is too good to waste.

1/2	cup olive oil
2	tablespoons lemon juice
1	tablespoon honey
1	tablespoon soy sauce
2	tablespoons chopped parsley
1	tablespoon Cajun seasoning
1	pound uncooked large shrimp, peeled, deveined

Wine Suggestion
California
Chardonnay

Combine the olive oil, lemon juice, honey, soy sauce, parsley and seasoning in a 9x13-inch baking dish; mix well. Add the shrimp, mixing to coat well. Marinate in the refrigerator for 1 hour or longer. Bake at 450 degrees for 10 minutes or until shrimp are cooked through.

SHRIMP AND VEGETABLES EN CROUTE

Serves 6 to 8

A winning combination of great taste and a beautiful presentation!

1   sheet frozen puff pastry
2   (3½x6-inch) slices Swiss cheese
18 large shrimp, peeled, deveined
    Salt and pepper to taste
12 ounces fresh mushrooms, sliced
1   medium onion, sliced
¼   teaspoon minced garlic
2   tablespoons butter
2   tablespoons dry white wine
¼   teaspoon dillweed
1½ cups broccoli flowerets, blanched
1   egg, beaten

Wine Suggestion
French Chablis

Thaw the pastry for 20 minutes. Roll into an 11x15-inch rectangle on a floured surface. Arrange the Swiss cheese down 1 side of the pastry. Arrange 3 rows of 6 shrimp over the cheese; sprinkle with salt and pepper. Sauté the mushrooms, onion and garlic in the butter in a skillet. Add the wine and dillweed. Cook until the liquid evaporates. Spoon over the shrimp. Top with the broccoli. Brush the edges of the pastry with a mixture of egg and water. Fold the pastry to enclose the filling; seal the edges. Brush with the egg mixture; slash the top with a sharp knife. Place on a baking sheet. Bake at 425 degrees for 20 to 25 minutes or until golden brown.

CIOPPINO

Serves 3 to 4

This is a great dish for Christmas Eve supper, with crisp garlic bread and a green salad.

¼   cup chopped green bell pepper
2   tablespoons chopped onion
1   clove of garlic, minced
1   tablespoon vegetable oil
1   (16-ounce) can tomatoes
1   (8-ounce) can tomato sauce
½   cup dry red wine
2   tablespoons chopped parsley
¼   teaspoon each basil and oregano
½   teaspoon salt
⅛   teaspoon pepper
8   ounces frozen cod filets, thawed
8   ounces monkfish, sea bass or tilapia
8   ounces frozen peeled shrimp, deveined
8   ounces clams with juice

Wine Suggestions
Italian Bardolino or
California
Chardonnay

Sauté the green pepper, onion and garlic in the oil in a saucepan for 5 minutes or until tender. Add the tomatoes, tomato sauce, wine, parsley, basil, oregano, salt and pepper. Simmer, covered, for 20 minutes. Cut the fish into 2-inch pieces. Add to the saucepan. Simmer for 5 minutes. Add the shrimp and undrained clams. Simmer for 3 minutes longer or until the shrimp are pink.

SEAFOOD STIR-FRY

Serves 4

Assemble the ingredients for this dish in advance and cook it just at serving time. Serve it from the wok over a bed of white rice; sprinkle the servings with chopped green onions.

4	scallions, chopped
3	tablespoons catsup
3	tablespoons chili sauce
3	tablespoons sherry
3	tablespoons soy sauce
2	teaspoons sugar
1/2	teaspoon salt
1	clove of garlic, minced
3	tablespoons minced ginger
2	tablespoons olive oil
1	pound fresh shrimp
1	pound fresh scallops

Wine Suggestions
White Rhine-style
wine such as
Viogniere or
Marsanne

Combine the scallions, catsup, chili sauce, wine, soy sauce, sugar and salt in a bowl; mix well and set aside.

Stir-fry the garlic and ginger in the oil in a wok or skillet over high heat. Add the shrimp and scallops. Stir-fry for 3 to 4 minutes. Add the catsup mixture. Cook for 3 to 5 minutes or until heated through.

SEAFOOD COQUILLES

Serves 4 or 5

Serve this with buttered broccoli spears and French rolls for an easy and light main course, or with wooden picks for a delicious appetizer.

1	(12-ounce) package frozen scallops, thawed, or 1 pound bay scallops
1	(10-ounce) package frozen cooked shrimp, thawed, drained
8	ounces mushrooms, sliced
2	(10-ounce) cans cream of shrimp soup
1	tablespoon grated lemon rind
1	tablespoon chopped chives
	Grated Parmesan cheese

Wine Suggestion
French Chablis

Combine the scallops, shrimp, mushrooms, soup, lemon rind and chives in a bowl; mix gently. Spoon about 1 cup of mixture into individual baking ramekins or shells; place on a baking sheet. Bake at 400 degrees for 15 minutes. Top with cheese. Bake for 2 to 3 minutes longer.

Family Favorites

ASPARAGUS AND PROSCIUTTO SANDWICHES

Serves 8

Serve as an appetizer or a light lunch in the spring when fresh asparagus is available.

24 fresh asparagus spears
4 English muffins, split, toasted
   Softened butter
8 slices prosciutto
   Salt and pepper to taste
8 slices Colby cheese

Cut the asparagus into 4-inch spears. Steam until tender; set aside. Spread the muffin halves with butter. Layer 1 slice of prosciutto and 3 asparagus spears on each muffin half; sprinkle with salt and pepper. Top with the cheese. Place on a baking sheet. Bake at 350 degrees for 5 to 10 minutes or until the cheese melts. Serve immediately.

BACON AND TURKEY CLUB SANDWICH

Serves 6

A sandwich that is a meal in itself and sure to please everyone.

4 cups thinly sliced cabbage
1/2 cup reduced-fat mayonnaise
1 tablespoon cider vinegar
2 teaspoons sugar
1/4 teaspoon salt
1/4 teaspoon pepper
10 slices turkey bacon
1 round loaf sourdough bread
2 plum tomatoes, sliced
8 ounces thinly sliced smoked turkey breast

Combine the cabbage, mayonnaise, vinegar, sugar, salt and pepper in a bowl; mix well. Let stand for 30 minutes.

Heat a skillet sprayed with nonstick cooking spray over medium-low heat. Add the bacon 1/2 at a time. Cook until crisp, turning frequently; drain.

Cut the bread into halves horizontally. Remove the soft center, reserving 1/2-inch shells. Spoon half the cabbage mixture into the bottom half of the bread. Layer with the bacon, tomatoes, turkey and remaining cabbage mixture. Top with the remaining bread; press lightly. Cut into 6 wedges to serve.

CHICKEN AND AVOCADO MELT

Serves 4

The sourdough bread is necessary to the subtle flavor of this hot sandwich.

1/2　cup mayonnaise or creamy salad dressing
3　tablespoons minced cilantro
1　tablespoon fresh lime juice
4　(1-inch) slices firm sourdough bread
4　(6-ounce) chicken breast filets
2　tablespoons vegetable oil
1　large tomato, cut into 8 slices
1　medium avocado, sliced
1　cup coarsely shredded Monterey Jack cheese

Combine the mayonnaise, 2 tablespoons of the cilantro and lime juice in a bowl; mix well. Toast the bread on both sides. Spread 1 side of each slice with the mayonnaise mixture.

Rinse the chicken and pat dry. Coat with the oil; place on a rack in a broiler pan. Broil 3 to 4 inches from the heat source for 15 minutes or until tender, turning once. Place on the prepared toasted bread; top with the tomato and avocado. Place in a broiler pan; sprinkle with the cheese. Broil until the cheese melts. Sprinkle with the remaining 1 tablespoon cilantro.

GRILLED CRAB SANDWICHES

Serves 6

A special lunch sandwich that is also quick and easy.

6　English muffins, split, lightly toasted
1/2　cup butter or margarine, softened
1　pound crab meat or 3 (6-ounce) cans crab meat
1/2　cup shredded Cheddar cheese
1/2　cup chopped black olives
1/4　cup chopped parsley
1/4　cup mayonnaise
1　tablespoon lemon juice
1/4　teaspoon hot pepper sauce

Spread the cut sides of the muffins with butter. Combine the crab meat, cheese, olives, parsley, mayonnaise, lemon juice and pepper sauce in a bowl; mix well. Spread on the muffins; place on a baking sheet. Bake at 350 degrees for 15 minutes or until heated through.

BAKED STUFFED BREAD

Serves 6

A colorful and tasty treat for lunch or a family supper.

2   cloves of garlic, minced
1/4   cup butter
2   (10-ounce) packages frozen chopped spinach, thawed, drained
1/2   cup grated Parmesan cheese
1   round loaf bread
8   ounces Swiss cheese, thinly sliced
1   (3 to 4-ounce) package sliced pepperoni
1   red bell pepper, chopped
2   tablespoons grated Parmesan cheese
      Olive oil

Sauté the garlic in half the butter in a skillet until tender but not brown. Add the remaining butter, spinach and 1/2 cup Parmesan cheese; mix well.

Slice off and reserve the top of the bread. Hollow out the bread, leaving a shell. Layer the Swiss cheese, spinach mixture, pepperoni and bell pepper 1/3 at a time in the prepared shell; top with 2 tablespoons Parmesan cheese. Replace the top of the bread; brush with olive oil. Wrap in foil. Bake at 350 degrees for 25 minutes or until heated through. Cut into wedges to serve.

ITALIAN POCKETS

Serves 8 to 10

This is a great idea for picnics and camping trips. The dressing and filling can be made in advance, chilled for up to two days and assembled at serving time.

The dressing

1/4   cup olive oil
3   tablespoons wine vinegar
1/4   teaspoon oregano
1/2   teaspoon salt
1/4   teaspoon pepper

The sandwiches

8   ounces Swiss cheese, thinly sliced, cut into strips
5 1/3 ounces Genoa salami, thinly sliced, cut into strips
1/2   cup thinly sliced celery
1/2   cup chopped red or green bell pepper
1   cup sliced black olives
1/4   cup sliced green onions
4   (or 5) pita bread rounds, cut into halves

Combine the olive oil, vinegar, oregano, salt and pepper in a bowl; mix well. Chill until serving time.

Combine the cheese, salami, celery, bell pepper, olives and green onions in a bowl; mix well. Chill, covered, until serving time. Combine the dressing and the filling in a bowl; mix well. Stuff into pita halves to serve.

SUBMARINE SANDWICHES

Serves 12

A great favorite at tailgate parties!

The dressing

1/2	cup red vinegar
1	cup vegetable oil
1/4	teaspoon parsley
2	tablespoons sugar
1/4	teaspoon each basil and oregano
1/8	teaspoon garlic salt
1	teaspoon each salt and pepper

The sandwiches

2	loaves French bread
1	pound each bologna, hard salami, provolone cheese and pepperoni, sliced
1/2	head lettuce, chopped
2	tomatoes, thinly sliced

Combine the vinegar, oil, parsley, sugar, basil, oregano, garlic salt, salt and pepper in a blender container; process until smooth. Chill for several hours.

Slice the bread into halves horizontally. Layer the bologna, salami, provolone, pepperoni, lettuce and tomatoes on the bottom halves of the bread. Drizzle with the desired amount of the dressing; replace the tops of the loaves. Slice into servings.

STROMBOLI SANDWICHES

Serves 6

Prepare stromboli sandwiches in advance for football outings. Heat them in the oven or microwave and take them along in an insulated carrier.

1	pound ground beef
1	tablespoon finely chopped onion
1/2	cup tomato sauce
1/2	cup catsup
2	tablespoons grated Parmesan cheese
1/4	teaspoon fennel seeds
1/8	teaspoon oregano
1/2	teaspoon garlic powder
2	tablespoons margarine, softened
1/4	teaspoon garlic powder
1/2	teaspoon paprika
6	Kaiser rolls or hamburger buns, split
6	slices mozzarella cheese

Brown the ground beef with the onion in a heated skillet, stirring until the ground beef is crumbly; drain. Add the tomato sauce, catsup, Parmesan cheese, fennel seeds, oregano and 1/2 teaspoon garlic powder; mix well. Simmer for 20 minutes.

Combine the margarine, 1/4 teaspoon garlic powder and paprika in a small bowl. Spread on the cut side of each roll top. Spoon the ground beef mixture onto the bottom halves of the rolls; top with the mozzarella cheese and roll tops. Wrap each in foil. Bake at 350 degrees for 15 minutes or until the cheese melts. May microwave each stromboli without the foil on High for 45 seconds.

AUTHENTIC CHEESE FONDUE

Serves 8

This is fun to serve and eat at a party or for a warm-up on a winter evening.

1	clove of garlic, cut into halves
1	teaspoon lemon juice
1	cup dry white wine
8	ounces Gruyère cheese, shredded
8	ounces Emmenthaler cheese, shredded
2	teaspoons cornstarch
2	tablespoons Kirsch or sherry
	Freshly grated nutmeg and pepper to taste
1	(or 2) loaves sourdough bread, cubed

Rub the inside of the fondue pot with the cut sides of the garlic. Add the lemon juice and wine. Cook over medium heat until bubbly. Reduce the heat to low. Add the cheese gradually, stirring constantly with a wooden spoon until melted. Blend the cornstarch with the liqueur in a small bowl. Add to the cheese mixture with the nutmeg and pepper; mix well. Cook for 2 to 3 minutes, stirring until thick and smooth; do not boil. Serve with bread cubes for dipping.

CHEESE SOUFFLE

Serves 4

This is a super accompaniment to ham and a delicious change from scrambled eggs.

1/4	cup flour
1/4	cup margarine
1	cup milk
1	cup shredded Cheddar or mozzarella cheese
2	egg yolks, beaten
4	egg whites
1/4	teaspoon cream of tartar

Melt margarine in a saucepan; blend in the flour and cook until bubbly. Stir in the milk. Cook until thickened and smooth, stirring constantly. Stir in the cheese until melted. Stir a small amount of the hot mixture into the egg yolks; stir the egg yolks into the hot mixture and remove from the heat. Beat the egg whites with the cream of tartar in a mixer bowl until stiff peaks form. Fold into the cheese mixture. Spoon into a greased 1½-quart baking dish. Set baking dish in a pan of warm water deep enough to come up side of dish at least 1 to 2 inches. Bake at 350 degrees for 30 to 40 minutes or until set.

BEEF BARBECUE

Serves 6 to 8

This old-fashioned barbecue can be made in advance and frozen until needed. Serve it on fresh bakery rolls.

1	(3 to 4-pound) blade or chuck roast
1	large onion, sliced
2	(10-ounce) cans tomato soup
1/2	cup catsup
1/2	cup vinegar
1/2	cup packed brown sugar
2	tablespoons Worcestershire sauce
2	bay leaves

Place the roast and onion in a baking dish. Bake, covered, at 325 degrees for 4 hours. Discard the bone and fat. Combine the soup, catsup, vinegar, brown sugar, Worcestershire sauce and bay leaves in a bowl; mix well. Pour over the roast. Bake, covered, for 1 hour longer; discard the bay leaves. Shred the beef into the sauce to serve.

BRITTANY BEEF

Serves 4 to 6

Serve with rice or noodles for a family fall or winter dinner.

3	slices bacon
1	clove of garlic, minced
1 1/2	pounds round steak
1/2	(10-ounce) can consommé
1/2	cup dry red wine
1/2	cup chopped carrot
1	small white onion, chopped
4	peppercorns
2	whole cloves
2	bay leaves

Cook the bacon in a skillet until brown but not crisp. Remove the bacon and cut into 1-inch pieces, reserving the drippings in the skillet. Add the garlic to the drippings. Sauté briefly. Cut the steak into serving pieces; coat with flour. Brown on both sides in the bacon drippings; remove to a baking dish. Add the bacon, consommé, wine, carrot, onion, peppercorns, cloves and bay leaves to the baking dish. Bake, covered, at 300 degrees for 2 to 2 1/2 hours or until tender; discard the bay leaves.

SOUTHWESTERN LASAGNA

Serves 8 to 12

Delicious any time of the year with a salad of greens, jicama and citrus fruit.

3	tablespoons flour
3	tablespoons melted butter
1¼	cups milk
½	teaspoon cumin
½	teaspoon oregano
½	teaspoon salt
1	cup sour cream
2½	cups chopped cooked chicken
12	(7-inch) flour tortillas
3	(10-ounce) packages frozen chopped spinach, thawed, drained
1	cup shredded Monterey Jack cheese
1	egg
¼	cup flour
¼	cup grated Parmesan cheese
1	teaspoon salt
½	teaspoon pepper
3	cups shredded Monterey Jack cheese
1	(16-ounce) jar medium salsa

Blend 3 tablespoons flour into the melted butter in a saucepan. Cook for several minutes. Add the milk, cumin, oregano and ½ teaspoon salt. Cook until thickened, stirring constantly. Stir in the sour cream and chicken.

Arrange 4 tortillas in an overlapping layer in the bottom and part of the way up the sides of an oiled 9x13-inch baking dish. Combine the spinach, 1 cup Monterey Jack cheese, egg, ¼ cup flour, Parmesan cheese, 1 teaspoon salt and pepper in a bowl. Spread in the prepared baking dish. Add a layer of 4 tortillas. Spread with the chicken mixture; sprinkle with half the remaining Monterey Jack cheese. Top with remaining tortillas, salsa and remaining Monterey Jack cheese. Bake, covered, with foil, at 350 degrees for 45 minutes. Bake, uncovered, for 15 minutes longer. Let stand for 5 to 10 minutes before serving.

MEXICAN LASAGNA

Serves 6

A great family meal to prepare in advance!

2   cups sour cream or half and half
1   egg, slightly beaten
1/2 cup chopped black olives
1 1/2 pounds ground beef
1   cup beer
1   envelope taco seasoning mix
1   (8-ounce) can tomato sauce
6   (to 8) flour tortillas
2   cups shredded Cheddar cheese
2   cups shredded Monterey Jack cheese
1   (4-ounce) can chopped green chilies

Combine the sour cream, egg and olives in a small bowl; mix well and set aside. Brown the ground beef in a skillet, stirring until crumbly; drain. Add the beer and taco seasoning mix. Simmer for 5 minutes. Add the tomato sauce. Simmer for 5 minutes or until slightly thickened.

Spread a small amount of the ground beef mixture in a 9x11-inch baking dish; top with 1/3 of the tortillas. Layer half the remaining beef mixture, half the sour cream mixture, 1/3 of the cheeses, half the remaining tortillas, the remaining ground beef mixture, remaining sour cream mixture, half of the remaining cheeses and the green chilies in the prepared dish. Top with the remaining tortillas and cheese. Bake, covered, at 350 degrees for 30 minutes.

VEGETABLE LASAGNA

Serves 4

The meat lovers in your family will never miss the meat in this flavorful dish.

2   eggs
1   pound dry curd cottage cheese or ricotta cheese
1   (10-ounce) package frozen chopped spinach, thawed, drained
1/4 teaspoon onion powder
1/4 teaspoon garlic powder
1/4 teaspoon salt
1/4 teaspoon pepper
     Uncooked lasagna noodles
1   (16-ounce) jar spaghetti sauce with mushrooms
1   pound mozzarella cheese, shredded

Beat the eggs in a mixer bowl. Add the cottage cheese; mix well. Stir in the spinach, onion powder, garlic powder, salt and pepper. Layer the uncooked noodles, spinach mixture, spaghetti sauce and mozzarella cheese 1/2 at a time in a greased baking pan. Bake at 400 degrees for 1 hour.

MOZZARELLA BEEF WHIRL

Serves 5

Kids love this great supper dish. Serve it with pasta tossed with garlic butter and a salad.

1½ pounds ground beef
½ cup soft bread crumbs
1 egg, slightly beaten
1 tablespoon prepared mustard
¼ cup minced onion
1½ teaspoons salt
⅛ teaspoon pepper
6 ounces mozzarella cheese, shredded
1 teaspoon parsley flakes
¾ cup catsup
¾ cup water
1 tablespoon Worcestershire sauce

Combine the ground beef, bread crumbs, egg, mustard, onion, salt and pepper in a bowl; mix well. Pat into a 10x14-inch rectangle on waxed paper. Sprinkle with the cheese and parsley flakes. Roll from the narrow side to enclose the filling. Place in a baking dish. Combine the catsup, water and Worcestershire sauce in a bowl; mix well. Pour over the roll. Bake at 375 degrees for 1 hour and 10 minutes.

SWEDISH MEATBALLS

Serves 6

The best, most flavorful and juicy meatballs. If you roll them in enough flour for the browning step, you may not need the additional flour to thicken the gravy.

1 cup bread crumbs
½ cup milk
8 ounces ground beef
8 ounces ground lean pork
1 egg, beaten
1 medium apple, peeled, grated
1 medium onion, grated
1½ teaspoons salt
¼ teaspoon pepper
½ cup flour
3 tablespoons vegetable oil
1½ cups beef broth
½ cup milk

Soak the bread crumbs in ½ cup milk in a bowl. Add the ground beef, ground pork, egg, apple, onion, salt and pepper; mix well. Shape into meatballs. Sift the flour onto a plate; roll the meatballs in the flour, reserving 1½ tablespoons of the floor.

Brown the meatballs on all sides in the oil in a skillet large enough to hold them in a single layer. Drain all but 3 tablespoons of the drippings. Stir in the reserved flour. Add the beef broth. Simmer, covered, for 10 minutes. Add ½ cup milk. Cook until heated through. Serve over noodles or mashed potatoes.

STUFFED CABBAGE LEAVES

Serves 8

This requires some advance preparation, but it can be done a day in advance and chilled until time to bake. Let stand until room temperature before baking.

The cabbage

1	large head cabbage
	Salt to taste
2	cups chopped mushrooms
3	tablespoons butter
2	cups chopped cooked ham
3/4	cup cooked rice
2	tablespoons chopped chives
1	cup chicken broth

The sauce

1/2	cup coarsely chopped onion
1/4	cup coarsely chopped celery
1/4	cup coarsely chopped green bell pepper
3	tablespoons butter or margarine
2 1/2	cups canned tomatoes
	Salt and pepper to taste
1 1/2	tablespoons cornstarch
3	tablespoons cold water

Discard the outer leaves of the cabbage and remove the bottom core with a sharp knife. Cook in salted boiling water to cover in a large saucepan for 5 to 7 minutes or until the leaves can be easily removed. Drain the saucepan and invert the cabbage to drain. Separate the leaves and pat dry. Sauté the mushrooms in the butter in a skillet. Add the ham, mushrooms, rice and chives; mix well. Spoon onto the cabbage leaves; roll the leaves to enclose the filling. Arrange in a baking dish. Add the broth. Bake, covered, for 1 hour, adding water if needed.

Sauté the onion, celery and green pepper in the butter in a saucepan for 5 minutes. Add the tomatoes. Bring to a boil; reduce the heat. Simmer for 15 minutes. Season with salt and pepper. Blend the cornstarch with the cold water in a cup. Add to the sauce. Cook until thickened, stirring constantly. Serve with the stuffed cabbage leaves.

CAULIFLOWER AND HAM CASSEROLE

Serves 4 to 6

The cauliflower in this dish is a nice change from potatoes.

1   head cauliflower, cut into bite-sized pieces
2   cups chopped cooked ham
4   ounces fresh mushrooms
2   tablespoons flour
2   tablespoons melted butter or margarine
1   cup milk
4   slices American cheese, chopped
1/2 cup sour cream
     Buttered bread crumbs or cracker crumbs

Cook the cauliflower in water in a saucepan just until tender; drain. Combine with the ham and mushrooms in a 1½-quart baking dish.

Blend the flour into the melted butter in a saucepan. Cook for several minutes. Add the milk gradually. Cook until thickened, stirring constantly. Stir in the cheese until melted. Add the sour cream; mix well. Spoon over the ham and cauliflower mixture; top with bread crumbs. Bake at 350 degrees for 30 minutes.

PORK CHOPS WITH AMBER RICE

Serves 6

Families love this easy combination of tender pork chops and wonderfully flavored rice.

1   cup uncooked brown rice or mixture of brown rice and wild rice
1   cup orange juice
1/2 cup water
1   (10-ounce) can chicken and stars soup
6   lean medium-thick pork chops
     Salt and pepper to taste

Sprinkle the rice into a 9x13-inch baking dish. Add the orange juice, water and soup; mix well. Bake, covered with foil, at 350 degrees for 30 minutes. Arrange the pork chops over the rice; sprinkle with salt and pepper. Bake, covered, for 20 minutes. Bake, uncovered, for 30 to 35 minutes or until the chops are tender and the liquid is absorbed.

ROASTED CHICKEN

Serves 4

Bake potatoes and a vegetable casserole with the chicken for an easy meal that is all ready at the same time. For an even simpler version, you can omit the garlic and vegetables placed in the cavity for roasting.

1   (3-pound) chicken
1   (or 2) cloves of garlic, sliced
     Chopped carrot, onion and celery

Remove the fat from the chicken and cut the fat into strips. Arrange the garlic slices between the skin and the meat of the chicken; replace the skin. Place the carrot, onion and celery in the cavity. Place in a roasting pan. Arrange the strips of fat over the breast and legs of the chicken. Roast at 350 degrees for 1 to 1¼ hours or until cooked through.

CHEESY TURKEY AND VEGETABLE PIE

Serves 5 to 8

A perfect one-dish meal for brunches and lunches!

1   unbaked (9-inch) pie shell or 1 recipe (1 crust) Pie Pastry (page 150)
1   cup broccoli flowerets
1   cup sliced carrots
1   bunch green onions, sliced
8   ounces fresh mushrooms, sliced
1   small zucchini, sliced
¼   teaspoon garlic powder
1   tablespoon butter
4   medium slices honey-baked turkey breast
4   slices Colby cheese
4   slices brick cheese
1   medium tomato, sliced
8   ounces sharp Cheddar cheese, shredded

Prick the pie shell. Bake at 350 degrees for 10 minutes. Steam the broccoli and carrots. Sauté the green onions, mushrooms and zucchini with the garlic powder in the butter in a skillet. Layer the turkey, Colby cheese, broccoli and carrots, brick cheese, sautéed vegetables, tomato and Cheddar cheese in the pie shell. Bake for 50 minutes or until the pastry is golden brown.

TURKEY ENCHILADA CASSEROLE

Serves 6 to 8

A good way to enhance those turkey leftovers. It can also be made with chicken.

4   (to 5) cups chopped or shredded cooked turkey or chicken
1   (10-ounce) can cream of mushroom soup
1   (10-ounce) can cream of chicken soup
1   cup sour cream
1/2 cup milk
3/4 cup chopped onion
1   can chopped green chilies
12   corn tortillas
4   cups shredded Cheddar cheese

Combine the turkey, soups, sour cream, milk, onion and green chilies in a bowl; mix well. Chill, covered, for 12 hours to overnight.

Spread a small layer of the turkey mixture in a baking dish. Layer the tortillas, the remaining turkey mixture and the cheese 1/2 at a time in the prepared dish. Bake at 325 degrees for 1 1/4 hours.

JACK CHEESE ENCHILADAS

Serves 4 to 6

A great make-ahead dish for the family, for parties or for tailgating.

2   cups shredded Monterey Jack cheese
3/4 cup chopped onion
1   (4-ounce) can chopped green chilies
12   flour tortillas
1/4 cup flour
1/4 cup melted butter
2   cups chicken broth
1   cup sour cream

Place 2 tablespoons of the cheese, 1 tablespoon of the onion and 1 teaspoon of the green chilies on each tortilla. Roll tortillas tightly to enclose the filling; arrange seam side down in a 9x13-inch baking dish.

Blend the flour into the melted butter in a saucepan. Add the chicken broth. Cook until thickened, stirring constantly; do not boil. Pour over the enchiladas. Bake at 425 degrees for 20 minutes. Sprinkle with the remaining 1/2 cup cheese. Bake just until the cheese melts. Dollop with the sour cream to serve.

NEW ENGLAND CORN AND OYSTER BAKE

Serves 10 to 16

It's not Christmas without this dish!

2   pints oysters
1/2 cup light cream
2   (16-ounce) cans cream-style corn
2   (16-ounce) cans whole kernel corn, drained
1/8 teaspoon Tabasco sauce
4   cups saltine cracker crumbs
1   cup melted butter
     Salt and pepper to taste

Drain the oysters, reserving the liquid. Chop the oysters or leave them whole as you prefer. Combine the reserved oyster liquid with the cream, corn and Tabasco sauce in a bowl; mix well. Toss the cracker crumbs with the melted butter in a bowl.

Alternate layers of the cracker crumbs, oysters and corn mixture in a 3-quart baking dish, sprinkling the layers with salt and pepper and ending with the cracker crumbs. Bake at 350 degrees for 1 hour.

BAKED LAYERED SPAGHETTI

Serves 6

This is easier to prepare in advance and serve than is traditional spaghetti. Add a salad and garlic bread for a vegetarian meal with fresh appeal.

4   teaspoons flour
2   tablespoons melted butter
3/4 cup whipping cream
1/4 cup milk
1 1/4 cups chopped green bell pepper
2   cups sliced mushrooms
2   small onions, chopped
2   tablespoons butter
1   (16-ounce) can stewed tomatoes
1/4 cup sliced black olives
8   ounces spaghetti, cooked, drained
1/2 cup grated Parmesan cheese

Blend the flour into 2 tablespoons melted butter in a saucepan. Add the cream and milk. Cook until thickened, stirring constantly.

Sauté the green pepper, mushrooms and onions in 2 tablespoons butter in a skillet. Stir in the tomatoes and olives.

Layer the spaghetti, white sauce, tomato sauce and Parmesan cheese in a 2 1/2-quart to 3-quart baking dish. Bake at 350 degrees for 30 to 45 minutes or at 300 degrees for 1 hour.

LIGHT POTATO PANCAKES

Serves 8

Delicious on cool fall evenings with roast pork, applesauce and sour cream!

3   eggs, beaten
2   tablespoons milk
2   tablespoons flour
1/4   teaspoon baking powder
1 1/4 teaspoons salt
8   potatoes, grated
1   onion, grated

Combine the eggs, milk, flour, baking powder and salt in a bowl; mix well. Stir in the potatoes and onion. Heat a nonstick or slightly oiled skillet to 350 degrees. Spoon the potato mixture a small amount at a time into the skillet. Cook until golden brown.

PIZZA STICKS

Serves 8

The kids love to help prepare—and eat—these treats.

1   (8-count) can soft breadsticks
24   thin pepperoni slices
2   tablespoons grated Parmesan cheese
1/2   teaspoon Italian seasoning
1/4   teaspoon garlic powder
1/2   cup pizza sauce

Separate the breadstick dough into 8 portions. Arrange 3 slices of pepperoni in a single layer on half of each breadstick. Fold the remaining half of the breadstick over the pepperoni. Press the edges to seal and twist the breadsticks. Place on an ungreased baking sheet. Sprinkle with a mixture of Parmesan cheese, Italian seasoning and garlic powder. Bake at 350 degrees for 15 to 20 minutes or until golden brown. Heat the pizza sauce in a saucepan. Serve with the pizza sticks for dipping. You may substitute ranch dressing for pizza sauce for variety.

VEGETABLES & STARCHES

*What was paradise, but a garden full of vegetables
and herbs and pleasure. Nothing there but delights.*

William Lawson

Vegetables & Starches

Asparagus Pie, 107

Chinese Asparagus, 107

Baked Beans Combo, 108

Baked Beets with Lemon Cream, 108

Steamed Brussels Sprouts and
Grapes, 109

Braised Shredded Red Cabbage, 109

Ginger-Glazed Carrots and
Turnips, 110

Eggplant and Rice Casserole, 111

Fresh Mushroom Casserole, 111

Bistro Onion Gratin, 112

Scalloped Onions and Almonds, 112

Parsnip Timbales with Parsley
Sauce, 113

Mexican Spinach Casserole, 114

Spinach Pie, 114

Stuffed Peppers with Goat
Cheese, 115

Fried Green Tomatoes with Milk
Gravy, 115

Tomatoes a la Provençal, 116

Zucchini and Tomato Pie, 116

Turnips Mary-Stuart, 117

Jarlsberg Vegetable Bake, 118

Oven-Roasted Vegetables, 118

Plum Tomatoes with Shallot Purée, 119

Golden Parmesan Potatoes, 119

Party Potatoes au Gratin, 120

Twice-Cooked Potatoes, 120

Bistro Potato Gratin, 121

Roasted New Potatoes with Lemon, 121

Potato Gratin with Cheese and
Ham, 122

Sweet Potato Casserole, 122

Sweet Potato Crunch, 123

Couscous, 123

Kugel, 124

Wild Rice with Pecans, 124

Rigatoni with Tomatoes and Vodka, 125

Mediterranean Pasta, 125

Shrimp and Artichoke Pasta, 126

Linguine with Broccoli and Tomato, 126

Linguine with Asparagus and
Mustard, 127

Turkey Tapenade, 127

Scallops with Tomato Basil Sauce, 128

Chicken Pasta with Sugar Snap
Peas, 128

Penne and Shrimp Quattro
Formaggio, 129

ASPARAGUS PIE

Serves 6

A lovely dish for the holidays because of its color.

16 ounces fresh or frozen asparagus spears, cooked al dente, drained
2 eggs
1 cup cottage cheese
1/4 cup melted butter
1/4 cup flour
1/2 teaspoon baking powder
1/4 teaspoon salt
1 cup sour cream
1 tomato, peeled, thinly sliced
1/4 cup grated Parmesan cheese

Arrange the asparagus spears in a spoke design in a greased 9-inch pie plate. Beat the eggs in a mixer bowl until frothy. Add the cottage cheese and butter. Beat until smooth. Stir in the flour, baking powder and salt. Stir in the sour cream until blended. Spoon the mixture over the asparagus. Top with tomato slices; sprinkle with Parmesan cheese. Bake at 350 degrees for 30 minutes or until set. Let stand for 10 minutes before slicing.

CHINESE ASPARAGUS

Serves 8

A great recipe to prepare during the spring when fresh asparagus is plentiful and reasonable in price!

1 tablespoon cornstarch
1 cup chicken broth
1 tablespoon soy sauce
2 teaspoons onion juice or 1/2 teaspoon onion powder
1/8 teaspoon pepper
2 pounds fresh asparagus, cut into diagonal slices
2 tablespoons vegetable oil
1/2 cup sliced water chestnuts
2 tablespoons slivered almonds

Combine the cornstarch, chicken broth, soy sauce, onion juice and pepper in a saucepan; mix well. Simmer for 2 minutes, stirring constantly. Stir-fry the asparagus in hot oil in a skillet over medium-high heat for 2 minutes. Add the cornstarch mixture; mix well. Cook for 2 to 3 minutes or until mixture is heated through, stirring frequently. Stir in water chestnuts and slivered almonds. Cook for 1 minute, stirring constantly. Serve immediately.

BAKED BEANS COMBO

Serve 10 to 12

The flavor of the dish is enhanced if the beans are prepared one day in advance.

8   slices bacon
4   onions, sliced
1   cup packed brown sugar
1   teaspoon prepared mustard
1   teaspoon salt
1/2   teaspoon garlic powder
1/2   cup cider vinegar
2   (15-ounce) cans Great Northern beans, drained
1   (16-ounce) can green lima beans, drained
1   (16-ounce) can dark red kidney beans, drained
1   (28-ounce) can pork and beans, drained

Fry the bacon in a saucepan until crisp. Drain, reserving the pan drippings. Crumble the bacon. Combine the reserved pan drippings, onions, brown sugar, mustard, salt, garlic powder and vinegar in the same saucepan. Simmer, covered, for 20 minutes, stirring occasionally. Combine the onion mixture with the beans in a slow cooker; mix well. Cook on Medium for 2 hours.

BAKED BEETS WITH LEMON CREAM

Serves 6 to 8

Baking is the best way to cook beets in order to preserve their flavor and color.

8   (1 1/2-inch) beets
1   tablespoon butter
1   shallot, minced
1/4   cup dry white wine
1   cup whipping cream
4   teaspoons grated lemon rind
2 1/2   teaspoons fresh lemon juice, strained
    Salt and freshly ground white pepper to taste

Rinse the beets; trim the roots and tops. Place the beets flat side down in a shallow baking pan. Bake, tightly covered with foil, at 325 degrees for 1 1/2 hours or until the beets are tender. Cool slightly. Peel the beets. Cut into thin slices or julienne strips. Arrange in a shallow dish.

Melt the butter in a saucepan over low heat. Stir in the shallot. Cook for 2 minutes, stirring frequently. Stir in the wine. Cook until the liquid has been reduced to 2 tablespoons, stirring occasionally. Remove from the heat. Stir in the whipping cream. Bring just to the simmering point; do not boil. Stir in the lemon rind. Add the lemon juice gradually, whisking constantly to prevent curdling. Stir in the salt and white pepper. Spoon over the beets. Garnish with lemon zest.

STEAMED BRUSSELS SPROUTS AND GRAPES

Serves 6 to 8

Red grapes are a succulent, colorful counterpoint to Brussels sprouts.

2   pints fresh Brussels sprouts of uniform size
2   cups stemmed seedless red grapes
2½ tablespoons unsalted butter
1   tablespoon fresh lemon juice
½   teaspoon salt
¼   teaspoon freshly ground pepper

Rinse the Brussels sprouts, trim off and discard the tough outer leaves and cut a small X at the stem ends to speed cooking process. Place the sprouts in a steamer basket over boiling water. Steam, tightly covered, for 15 minutes or until tender. Add the grapes. Steam for 1 minute longer; drain well.

Place the Brussels sprouts and the grapes in a serving bowl. Add the butter, lemon juice, salt and pepper; toss until coated. Serve hot.

BRAISED SHREDDED RED CABBAGE

Serves 6 to 8

With red vegetables, the addition of a small amount of acid is needed to preserve their color; hence the sour apple, red wine and red wine vinegar were added.

1   large red onion, thinly sliced
3   tablespoons butter or vegetable oil
2   large cloves of garlic, crushed
6   cups shredded red cabbage
1   teaspoon salt
    Freshly ground pepper to taste
2   teaspoons caraway seeds
1   bay leaf
1   cooking apple, grated
¾   cup chicken broth
¾   cup red wine
1   tablespoon red wine vinegar
1   tablespoon sugar
¼   cup chopped fresh parsley

Sauté the red onion in butter in a saucepan until tender. Stir in the garlic. Sauté for 30 seconds. Stir in the cabbage, salt, pepper, caraway seeds, bay leaf, apple, broth, red wine, wine vinegar and sugar. Boil, covered, for 10 to 15 minutes or until cabbage is al dente, stirring occasionally. May add additional broth or water if needed. Discard the bay leaf; adjust the seasonings. Toss with the parsley.

GINGER-GLAZED CARROTS AND TURNIPS

Serves 3 to 4

In French restaurants, vegetables that are carved into oval shapes are popular because they cook evenly and look elegant. Serve this dish with roast duck or chicken.

2¹/₂   cups chicken or vegetable stock
3   tablespoons minced peeled fresh ginger
4   medium carrots
3   small turnips
     Salt to taste
1¹/₂   teaspoons sugar
3   tablespoons unsalted butter
2   tablespoons minced peeled fresh ginger
     Freshly ground pepper to taste

Bring the stock and 3 tablespoons ginger to a boil in a saucepan; reduce heat. Cook over medium-high heat for 30 minutes. Strain, pressing the ginger through the strainer. Cut the carrots into 1¹/₂-inch lengths. Trim each piece into an oval, rounding off the corners. Cut the turnips into quarters. Trim each quarter into an oval shape. Arrange the carrots in a single layer in a saucepan. Add 1¹/₄ cups ginger-flavored stock or just enough to cover. Add the salt, 1 teaspoon of the sugar, 2 tablespoons of the butter and 2 tablespoons ginger. Bring to a boil; reduce the heat to medium. Simmer for 15 minutes or until the carrots are tender. Cool. Remove the carrots to a bowl.

Boil the remaining carrot liquid until reduced to ¹/₃ cup. Strain, pressing the ginger through the strainer. Return the liquid and carrots to the saucepan.

Arrange the turnips in a single layer in another saucepan. Add the remaining ginger-flavored stock or just enough to cover the turnips. Add the salt, ¹/₂ teaspoon sugar and 1 tablespoon butter. Bring to a boil; reduce the heat to medium. Simmer for 7 minutes or until the turnips are tender-crisp. Remove the turnips to a bowl.

Boil the remaining turnip liquid until reduced to ¹/₄ cup. Combine the turnip liquid and the turnips with the carrots; mix gently. Season with pepper. Cook over medium-high heat just until heated through, stirring frequently.

EGGPLANT AND RICE CASSEROLE

Serves 6

Serve with roasted leg of lamb for an elegant meal.

1	onion, chopped
1	green bell pepper, chopped
1/2	cup butter
1	cup uncooked rice
1	large eggplant, peeled, chopped
1	(14-ounce) can tomatoes
1/2	teaspoon basil
1/2	teaspoon oregano
2	cups beef bouillon
1/2	teaspoon pepper
3/4	teaspoon salt
	Hot pepper sauce to taste
1	cup shredded Cheddar cheese

Sauté the onion and green pepper in the butter in a saucepan until tender. Add the rice; mix well. Sauté until brown. Stir in the eggplant, tomatoes, basil, oregano, bouillon, pepper, salt and hot pepper sauce. Spoon into a greased 2-quart baking dish. Bake at 350 degrees for 30 minutes. Sprinkle with the cheese. Bake for 30 minutes.

FRESH MUSHROOM CASSEROLE

Serves 4 to 6

Serve as a side dish with roast beef or chicken. The recipe may be halved or doubled according to your needs.

2	small onions, chopped
12	(to 16) ounces mushrooms, finely chopped
2	eggs, slightly beaten
3/4	cup milk
3/4	cup half and half
3/4	teaspoon salt
1/4	teaspoon pepper
1/2	cup unseasoned fine dry bread crumbs
1/2	(to 2/3) cup shredded Cheddar cheese
	Red or green bell pepper rings
	Chopped fresh parsley

Spray a skillet with nonstick cooking spray. Sauté onions and mushrooms in prepared skillet over medium-high heat for 10 minutes or until most of the liquid has evaporated. Stir in mixture of eggs, milk, half and half, salt, pepper and bread crumbs. Spoon into a greased 1-quart baking dish. Sprinkle with the cheese; top with red or green pepper rings. Bake at 350 degrees for 45 minutes or until brown. Sprinkle with chopped fresh parsley.

BISTRO ONION GRATIN

Serves 8

For this gratin, find the freshest sweet onions possible to use—preferably Vidalia—and don't skimp on the nutmeg and pepper.

2   pounds large white onions, cut into ¹/₂-inch slices
     Salt to taste
3   tablespoons Crème Fraîche (page 194) or whipping cream
     Freshly grated nutmeg
     Freshly ground pepper to taste

Place the onions in a saucepan filled with boiling salted water. Cook for 10 minutes or just until onions are tender; drain. Combine the onions with the Crème Fraîche in a bowl; mix well. Season with the nutmeg, salt and pepper. Spoon into a medium gratin dish or 10-inch round baking dish. Bake at 375 degrees for 30 minutes or until onions are soft and golden brown. Serve immediately.

SCALLOPED ONIONS AND ALMONDS

Serves 6 to 8

To prevent whole onions from breaking apart as they cook, make an incision in the form of a cross at the root end, and then proceed with the recipe.

8   (to 10) small onions, peeled
     Salt to taste
1   cup chopped celery
¹/₄ cup melted butter
3   tablespoons flour
1   teaspoon salt
¹/₈ teaspoon pepper
1   cup milk
¹/₂ cup light cream
¹/₄ cup freshly grated Parmesan cheese
¹/₂ cup blanched slivered almonds
     Paprika to taste

Cook the onions in boiling salted water in a saucepan until tender; drain. Cook the celery in boiling salted water in a saucepan until tender; drain. Combine the butter, flour, 1 teaspoon salt and pepper in a saucepan; mix well. Cook over low heat until bubbly, stirring constantly. Stir in milk, cream and Parmesan cheese. Cook until thickened, stirring constantly. Layer the onions, celery and almonds in a buttered casserole. Spoon the cream sauce over the prepared layers. Sprinkle with the paprika. Bake at 350 degrees for 30 minutes or until bubbly and brown.

PARSNIP TIMBALES WITH PARSLEY SAUCE

Serves 4 or 5

An unusual and delicious side dish. Excellent with duck, pork and chicken.

The timbales

1½ pounds parsnips
    Salt to taste
⅔ cup whipping cream, at room temperature
3 eggs
    Freshly ground pepper to taste
    Freshly grated nutmeg to taste

The parsley sauce

4 medium shallots, minced
1 bay leaf
½ cup dry white wine
1 cup chicken or vegetable stock
2 cups whipping cream
    Salt and freshly ground black pepper to taste
1 cup packed fresh parsley
    Cayenne pepper to taste

Butter one 20-ounce, four 5-ounce or five 4-ounce timbale molds. Peel and cut the parsnips crosswise into ½-inch slices. Bring the parsnips, salt and enough water to cover to a boil in a saucepan; reduce heat. Simmer for 20 minutes or until tender; drain. Process the parsnips in the food processor until puréed. Measure 2 cups puréed parsnips into saucepan; discard remaining purée. Bring to a boil, stirring constantly; reduce heat. Simmer for 5 minutes or until excess liquid has evaporated, stirring constantly. Stir in the whipping cream. Bring to a boil; reduce heat. Simmer until the cream is absorbed and the mixture is reduced to 2 cups in volume, stirring frequently. Pour into a bowl. Cool for 7 minutes. Whisk the eggs in a bowl until blended. Gradually whisk in the puréed mixture. Season with the salt, pepper and nutmeg. Spoon into the desired number of molds; cover with buttered foil. Place the molds in a roasting pan. Fill the pan with enough water to come half way up sides of the molds. Bake at 375 degrees for 1½ hours. Cool on a wire rack for 5 minutes.

Bring the shallots, bay leaf and white wine to a boil in a heavy saucepan. Add the stock; mix well. Bring to a boil; reduce the heat to medium-high. Cook until liquid is reduced to ½ cup, stirring frequently. Add the whipping cream, salt and black pepper; mix well. Bring to a boil, stirring constantly. Reduce the heat to medium. Cook for 7 minutes or until thickened, stirring frequently. Strain, pressing seasonings against the side of the strainer. May store the sauce in the refrigerator at this point for 1 day. Process the parsley and a small amount of the sauce in a food processor until puréed. Stir into the remaining sauce. Add the cayenne pepper; mix well. Cook just until heated through, stirring constantly.

Loosen timbales from molds with a thin-bladed knife; invert onto serving plate. Spoon 2 to 3 tablespoons of the parsley sauce around each timbale. Pass the remaining sauce.

MEXICAN SPINACH CASSEROLE

Serves 6 to 8

Zesty flavor!

2   (10-ounce) packages frozen chopped spinach
1/4 cup melted butter
2   tablespoons flour
1/2 (12-ounce) can evaporated milk
2   tablespoons chopped onion, sautéed
8   ounces jalapeño cheese, shredded
3/4 teaspoon each celery salt and garlic salt
     Pepper to taste
1   teaspoon Worcestershire sauce
     Buttered bread crumbs

Cook the spinach in a saucepan using the package directions. Drain and squeeze the moisture from the spinach, reserving 1/2 cup of the liquid. Combine the butter and flour in a saucepan; mix well. Stir in the reserved spinach liquid, evaporated milk and onion. Cook until thickened, stirring constantly. Stir in the cheese, celery salt, garlic salt, pepper and Worcestershire sauce. Cook until the cheese melts, stirring constantly. Stir in the spinach. Spoon into a greased baking dish; sprinkle with bread crumbs. Bake at 325 degrees for 45 minutes.

SPINACH PIE

Serves 6 to 8

A great side dish to serve during the fall and winter, or during the summer with grilled steaks. As a variation, bake in an 8-inch or 9-inch square baking pan, cut into squares and serve as an appetizer.

The pie shell

1   cup shredded Cheddar cheese
3/4 cup flour
1/2 teaspoon salt
1/4 teaspoon dry mustard
1/4 cup melted butter

The spinach filling

1   (10-ounce) package frozen chopped spinach, cooked, drained
1/2 cup each milk and half and half
1/2 cup finely chopped onion
1/4 cup chopped mushrooms
1   teaspoon salt
1/4 teaspoon nutmeg
     Pepper to taste
3   eggs, slightly beaten

Combine the cheese, flour, salt, dry mustard and butter in a bowl; mix well. Pat into a greased 9-inch pie plate sprayed with nonstick cooking spray.

Combine the spinach, milk, half and half, onion, mushrooms, salt, nutmeg and pepper in a bowl; mix well. Stir in 1/2 of the eggs; mix well. Add the remaining eggs; mix well. Spoon into the prepared pie plate. Bake at 400 degrees for 15 minutes. Reduce the temperature to 325 degrees. Bake for 20 to 25 minutes or until set. Let stand for several minutes before serving.

STUFFED PEPPERS WITH GOAT CHEESE

Serves 4

Serve as a side dish with roast lamb.

4   large green bell peppers
12 ounces montrachet or other soft mild goat cheese, cut into 8 pieces
1   tablespoon chopped Italian parsley
16 large fresh basil leaves
2   large plum tomatoes, cut into 1/4-inch slices
    Freshly ground pepper to taste
1/4 teaspoon thyme
1   tablespoon olive oil
1/2 cup dry white wine

Slice tops from the bell peppers; reserve the tops. Remove and discard the cores and seeds. Cut a thin slice from the bottom of each green pepper to allow pepper to stand upright; leave bottom intact for filling. Place 1 piece of cheese in each green pepper. Top with 1/2 teaspoon parsley, 2 of the basil leaves, tomato slices, pepper, thyme and 2 more basil leaves. Drizzle with 1/2 teaspoon olive oil. Top with the remaining cheese, pepper and remaining parsley. Replace tops; rub green peppers with the remaining olive oil. Place in shallow baking dish; pour the wine around the green peppers. Bake at 350 degrees for 40 minutes or until the green peppers are tender. Serve immediately.

FRIED GREEN TOMATOES WITH MILK GRAVY

Serves 4 to 6

Great dish to serve in the summer when tomatoes are plentiful!

4   green tomatoes, cut into 1/2-inch slices
2   eggs, beaten
    Dry bread crumbs
3   (to 4) tablespoons bacon grease
    Flour
1   cup warm milk
    Salt and pepper to taste

Dip the green tomatoes in the eggs in a bowl; coat with the bread crumbs. Fry the tomato slices in the bacon grease in a skillet until brown on both sides, turning once. Remove to a warm platter. Measure the pan drippings. Combine with 1 tablespoon flour for each tablespoon pan drippings in a skillet; mix well. Stir in the warm milk. Cook until thickened, stirring constantly. Season with salt and pepper. Serve the gravy with the tomatoes.

TOMATOES A LA PROVENCAL

Serves 8

The extra garlic makes this dish something special.

8   ripe tomatoes or 12 plum tomatoes
      Salt and freshly ground pepper to taste
8   cloves of garlic, chopped
1   cup fresh bread crumbs
      Finely chopped Italian parsley to taste
5   tablespoons olive oil

Cut the tomatoes crosswise into halves. Arrange the tomatoes cut side up in a large baking dish; do not remove the seeds or drain the tomatoes. Season with salt and pepper; sprinkle with the garlic. Top with a mixture of the bread crumbs and parsley; drizzle with the olive oil. Bake at 400 degrees for 1 hour or until the tomatoes are tender. Serve immediately.

ZUCCHINI AND TOMATO PIE

Serves 8

Serve as an entrée or as a side dish.

1   sheet frozen puff pastry, thawed
3   medium zucchini, thinly sliced
3   tablespoons butter
1/2   clove of garlic, minced, or 1/4 teaspoon garlic powder
1/4   teaspoon dillweed
1/8   teaspoon pepper
1   tomato, thinly sliced
3/4   cup shredded Monterey Jack cheese
3/4   cup shredded Cheddar cheese
2   teaspoons chopped fresh parsley

Press the puff pastry into a 9-inch pie plate. Seal edges; pierce with a fork. Sauté the zucchini in the butter in a skillet until tender. Stir in the garlic, dillweed and pepper. Spoon into the prepared pie plate. Arrange the tomato slices over the zucchini. Sprinkle with the cheeses and the parsley. Bake at 325 degrees for 45 to 50 minutes or until set.

TURNIPS MARY-STUART

Serves 6 to 8

Buy bunches of turnips with smooth, uncracked skins and firm roots that feel heavy for their size.

10 tablespoons melted unsalted butter
1/2 cup bacon drippings
6 tablespoons flour
1/2 cup freshly grated Parmesan cheese
3/4 teaspoon salt
1/2 teaspoon ginger
1/4 teaspoon dry mustard
1/4 teaspoon freshly ground pepper
1/4 teaspoon thyme, crushed
1/4 teaspoon rosemary, crushed
1/4 teaspoon freshly grated nutmeg
1 1/2 pounds medium turnips, peeled, sliced paper-thin

Brush a 9-inch glass pie plate with some of the melted butter. Combine the remaining butter with the bacon drippings in a bowl; mix well. Combine the flour, Parmesan cheese, salt, ginger, dry mustard, pepper, thyme, rosemary and nutmeg in a bowl; mix well. Spoon 1/4 cup of the flour mixture onto a plate.

Pick out the prettiest and most uniform turnip slices. Dip 1 into the butter mixture; press 1 side into the flour mixture on the plate. Lay the turnip slice floured side up in the center of the prepared pie plate. Repeat the process placing the slices, overlapping them slightly and working out from the center in concentric rings, to cover the bottom and side of the pie plate.

Continue layering the remaining turnip slices in slightly overlapping concentric rings. Brush each layer with some of the remaining butter mixture and sprinkle with the remaining flour mixture until all the turnips have been used.

Brush the butter mixture on the shiny side of a 9-inch square of foil. Place buttered side down on top of the turnips. Place a heavy 8-inch or 9-inch skillet on top of the foil; press firmly. Fill the skillet with pie weights or dried beans.

Bake at 450 degrees for 30 to 35 minutes or until the bottom and side are brown. Remove the pie plate from the oven; remove the skillet and discard the foil. Loosen the edges with a thin spatula. Let stand for 5 minutes. Invert onto a heated serving platter. Cut into wedges.

JARLSBERG VEGETABLE BAKE

Serves 6 to 8

Serve during the summer months when zucchini is so plentiful.

3   medium zucchini, sliced
1   cup sliced mushrooms
1/2   cup green bell pepper strips
1/2   cup sliced green onions
1   clove of garlic, minced
1/4   cup olive oil
1   cup cherry tomato halves
1/2   teaspoon salt
1/8   teaspoon pepper
2   cups shredded Jarlsberg cheese

Sauté the zucchini, mushrooms, green pepper, green onions and garlic in the olive oil in a skillet for 5 to 6 minutes or until the vegetables are tender. Stir in the tomatoes, salt and pepper. Layer the vegetable mixture and cheese alternately in a greased 1 1/2-quart baking dish until all the ingredients are used, ending with cheese. Bake at 350 degrees for 30 minutes.

OVEN-ROASTED VEGETABLES

Serves 4 to 6

Quick and easy to prepare!

10   unpeeled new potatoes, cut into quarters
1   cup peeled baby carrots
1   small onion, cut into wedges
1/4   cup olive oil
3   tablespoons lemon juice
3   cloves of garlic, minced
1   tablespoon minced fresh rosemary or 1 teaspoon dried rosemary
1   teaspoon salt
1/2   teaspoon pepper
1/2   small eggplant, cut into 1/2-inch slices
1   medium red or green bell pepper, cut into 1/2-inch strips

Arrange the new potatoes, carrots and onion in a 9x13-inch baking dish. Drizzle with a mixture of olive oil, lemon juice, garlic, rosemary, salt and pepper. Bake at 450 degrees for 30 minutes, stirring occasionally. Stir in the eggplant and bell pepper. Bake for 15 minutes. May substitute 1 teaspoon dried oregano for rosemary.

PLUM TOMATOES WITH SHALLOT PUREE

Serves 4

The tomatoes can also be served standing on their ends. Cut a thin slice off the bottom of the tomato so it will balance. Then cut off the top fourth of the tomato, reserving the top. Replace the top after stuffing the tomato.

1   pound shallots, peeled, cut into halves
3/4   cup butter
     Salt and freshly ground pepper to taste
8   plum tomatoes
2   teaspoons vegetable oil
1/2   cup whipping cream
2   teaspoons thinly sliced chives or parsley sprigs

Bring the shallots and enough water to cover to a boil in a saucepan. Boil for 2 minutes; drain. Melt the butter in a skillet over low heat. Stir in the shallots, salt and pepper. Cook, covered, for 20 minutes or until the shallots are tender, stirring frequently. Cut the tomatoes lengthwise into halves; scoop out the ribs and seeds with a melon baller. Arrange the tomatoes in a single layer in a greased baking dish. Season with salt and pepper; drizzle with the oil. Bake at 400 degrees for 10 minutes or just until tender. Invert the tomatoes to drain; pat dry with a paper towel. Return the tomatoes to the baking dish. Purée the shallots in a food processor. Combine the purée and whipping cream in a saucepan. Cook over low heat until the cream is absorbed, stirring constantly. Adjust the seasonings. Spoon the shallot purée into the tomatoes. Bake for 7 minutes or until the tomatoes are very tender. Garnish with chives or parsley sprigs. Serve hot or warm.

GOLDEN PARMESAN POTATOES

Serves 6 to 8

Great buffet dish anytime of the year!

1/3   cup melted butter
1/4   cup sifted flour
1/4   cup grated Parmesan cheese
3/4   teaspoon salt
1/4   teaspoon pepper
6   large potatoes, peeled
     Chopped fresh parsley to taste

Coat the bottom of a 9x13-inch baking dish with the melted butter. Combine the flour, cheese, salt and pepper in a food storage bag; mix well. Cut each potato into 8 wedges. Moisten the potatoes slightly with water. Shake 1/3 of the potatoes at a time in the flour mixture, tossing to coat. Arrange the potatoes in the prepared dish. Bake at 375 degrees for 1 hour or until brown on both sides, turning once. Sprinkle with parsley.

PARTY POTATOES AU GRATIN

Serves 15

A good dish to serve to large crowds. Serve with baked chicken or ham.

16 ounces mushrooms
3/4 cup butter
3/4 cup flour
4 cups milk
1 (10-ounce) can consommé
16 ounces sharp Cheddar cheese, shredded
1 tablespoon seasoned salt
1/4 teaspoon pepper
1 teaspoon Worcestershire sauce
2 (15-ounce) cans small white onions, drained
5 pounds red potatoes, cooked, peeled, cut into 1/2-inch pieces

Sauté the mushrooms in the butter in a large saucepan until light brown. Stir in the flour, milk and consommé. Cook until thickened, stirring constantly. Stir in the cheese, seasoned salt, pepper and Worcestershire sauce. Cook until smooth, stirring constantly. Remove from the heat. Add the onions and potatoes gradually; mix well. Spoon into a 4-quart baking pan. Chill, covered with foil, for 1 1/2 hours. Bake at 350 degrees for 1 to 1 1/2 hours or until brown and bubbly.

TWICE-COOKED POTATOES

Serves 12

May freeze these potatoes and reheat in the microwave. Add variety by including chopped broccoli, sliced mushrooms or chopped meat in the filling.

6 large potatoes, baked, cut into halves lengthwise
3 tablespoons skim milk, heated
1 teaspoon grated onion, sautéed
1 teaspoon salt
1 tablespoon horseradish
2 egg whites, stiffly beaten
1/2 cup grated hard cheese
   Paprika to taste

Scoop the potato pulp carefully into a mixer bowl, reserving the shells. Beat in the skim milk, onion, salt and horseradish until blended. Fold in the egg whites. Spoon into the reserved shells. Place on a baking sheet. Sprinkle with cheese and paprika. Broil until cheese melts.

BISTRO POTATO GRATIN

Serves 6 to 8

In France many cooks talk of the double-cooking method, in which you first cook the potatoes in a mixture of milk and water, discard the cooking liquid, and then bake the potatoes in a blend of cream and Gruyère cheese. It makes for a rich, delicious gratin.

3   pounds baking potatoes, peeled, thinly sliced
2   cups milk
2   cups water
4   cloves of garlic, minced
3/4 teaspoon salt
3   bay leaves
    Freshly ground nutmeg to taste
    Freshly ground pepper to taste
1   cup Crème Fraîche (page 194) or whipping cream
2   cups freshly shredded Gruyère cheese

Combine the potatoes, milk and water in a large saucepan; mix well. Stir in the garlic, salt and bay leaves. Bring to a boil over medium-high heat, stirring occasionally; reduce the heat to medium. Cook for 10 minutes or until the potatoes are tender-crisp, stirring occasionally; drain. Discard the bay leaves. Layer the potatoes, nutmeg, pepper, Crème Fraîche and cheese 1/2 at a time in a 13-inch baking dish. Bake at 375 degrees for 1 hour or until the potatoes are golden brown and crisp on top. Serve immediately.

ROASTED NEW POTATOES WITH LEMON

Serves 6

Lemon juice and grated lemon rind add a refreshing flavor to the new potatoes.

3   pounds small new potatoes, unpeeled, cut into quarters
     Salt and pepper to taste
1/4 cup unsalted butter
1/4 cup olive oil
6   tablespoons fresh lemon juice
2 1/2 teaspoons thyme, crushed
1 1/2 tablespoons grated lemon rind
3   tablespoons minced fresh parsley

Arrange the new potatoes in a buttered baking dish. Season with salt and pepper. Combine the butter and olive oil in a saucepan. Cook until blended, stirring occasionally. Stir in the lemon juice. Drizzle over the new potatoes, tossing to coat; sprinkle with thyme. Bake at 375 degrees for 1 hour. May prepare in advance to this point and complete the cooking process just before serving. Sprinkle with the lemon rind, tossing to coat. Bake for 20 minutes or until the potatoes are tender and golden brown. Sprinkle with parsley.

POTATO GRATIN WITH CHEESE AND HAM

Serves 6

Serve as a main course or as a side dish.

1   tablespoon unsalted butter
4   large baking potatoes, peeled, thinly sliced
5   medium-thick slices smoked ham, trimmed, cut into 1-inch strips
3   cups freshly shredded Swiss or Gruyère cheese
     Freshly grated nutmeg to taste
     Salt and freshly ground pepper to taste
3   tablespoons unsalted butter

Coat the inside of an oval porcelain baking dish with 1 tablespoon butter. Layer the potatoes, ham, cheese, nutmeg, salt, and pepper ½ at a time in the prepared dish. Dot with 3 tablespoons butter. Bake at 375 degrees for 50 minutes or until golden brown. Serve immediately.

SWEET POTATO CASSEROLE

Serves 10

Serve during the Thanksgiving and Christmas holidays. May be prepared one day in advance, refrigerated overnight and baked just before serving.

The topping

1   cup packed brown sugar
⅓   cup melted butter
½   cup flour
1   cup chopped pecans

The sweet potatoes

3   cups mashed cooked sweet potatoes
1   cup sugar
⅓   cup milk
2   eggs, beaten
½   cup butter, softened
1   teaspoon vanilla extract

Combine the brown sugar, butter, flour and pecans in a bowl; mix well. Set aside.

Combine the sweet potatoes, sugar, milk, eggs, butter and vanilla in a bowl; mix well. Spoon into a baking dish. Sprinkle the brown sugar topping over the sweet potatoes. Bake at 350 degrees for 35 minutes.

SWEET POTATO CRUNCH

Serves 12

A great holiday dish!

The topping

2 cups packed brown sugar
2 cups pecan pieces
1/4 cup butter, softened

The sweet potatoes

6 sweet potatoes, peeled, cooked
1 (8-ounce) can pineapple tidbits, drained
1/4 cup butter
1 cup packed brown sugar
1/4 cup cinnamon
2 cups miniature marshmallows

Combine the brown sugar and pecan pieces in a bowl; mix well. Add the butter 1 tablespoon at a time, mixing well after each addition. Set aside.

Process the sweet potatoes, pineapple, butter, brown sugar and cinnamon in a food processor or blender until smooth. Spoon into a 4-quart baking dish. Bake at 325 degrees for 20 minutes or until bubbly. Spread with the pecan topping; sprinkle with the marshmallows. Bake until brown.

COUSCOUS

Serves 4

Great side dish with chicken or beef.

1 1/2 cups chicken broth
2 tablespoons butter
1 cup couscous
1 tomato, seeded, chopped
1 cup canned chickpeas, drained
1/4 cup raisins
1/2 teaspoon cinnamon
1/2 teaspoon basil
1/2 teaspoon thyme
 Salt and pepper to taste

Bring the broth and butter to a boil in a saucepan. Stir in the couscous. Remove from heat. Cover. Let stand for 5 minutes. Stir in the tomato, chickpeas, raisins, cinnamon, basil and thyme. Season with salt and pepper. Spoon into a buttered baking dish. Bake, covered, at 350 degrees for 15 minutes.

KUGEL

Serves 12 to 20

Great for brunch!

4	tablespoons melted butter
4	eggs, slightly beaten
1	teaspoon vanilla extract
1	teaspoon cinnamon
2	(16-ounce) packages medium egg noodles, cooked, drained
16	ounces cottage cheese with pineapple
1	(12-ounce) jar pineapple preserves
1/4	cup sugar
1/2	cup sour cream
4	tablespoons melted butter
1	cup crushed cornflakes

Coat a 9x13-inch baking dish with 4 tablespoons butter. Combine the eggs, vanilla and cinnamon in a bowl; mix well. Pour over egg noodles in a bowl. Stir in the cottage cheese, preserves, sugar, sour cream and 4 tablespoons butter. Sprinkle with cornflake crumbs. Bake at 325 degrees for 1 hour or until light brown. Let stand for several minutes before serving. Serve plain or with additional sour cream.

WILD RICE WITH PECANS

Serves 6

Add shredded Cheddar cheese to make a main dish or add chopped green or red bell pepper, sliced mushrooms or sliced greens onions in place of, or in addition to, the celery for variety.

1	cup chopped pecans
1/4	cup butter
3	stalks celery, sliced
3	(to 4) cups cooked wild rice
1	teaspoon garlic salt
2	(to 3) tablespoons snipped fresh parsley

Sauté the pecans in the butter in a skillet until light brown. Stir in the celery. Sauté for 8 minutes or until tender-crisp. Add the wild rice, garlic salt and parsley; mix well. Cook until heated through, stirring constantly.

RIGATONI WITH TOMATOES AND VODKA

Serves 4

Just add a salad and crusty bread for a satisfying one-dish meal with a different flavor.

1   small onion, chopped
2   cloves of garlic, minced
1   tablespoon Italian seasoning
2   tablespoons butter
1   (16-ounce) can Italian plum tomatoes, chopped
1/2 cup vodka
3/4 cup whipping cream
1   cup grated Parmesan cheese
3   ounces prosciutto or ham, chopped
8   ounces rigatoni, cooked
    Salt and pepper to taste

Sauté the onion and garlic with the Italian seasoning in the butter in a large heavy skillet over medium-high heat for 4 minutes or until the onion is tender. Add the undrained tomatoes and vodka. Simmer for 5 minutes, stirring occasionally. Stir in the cream and 1/2 cup of the cheese. Simmer for 4 minutes or until slightly thickened. Add the prosciutto and pasta. Cook until heated through, stirring gently. Season with salt and pepper. Serve with the additional cheese.

MEDITERRANEAN PASTA

Serves 2 to 4

This pretty and spicy pasta dish is best when a vine-ripened tomato is used.

4   cloves of garlic, minced
2   tablespoons olive oil
1   large tomato, chopped
1/3 cup minced fresh parsley
1/4 teaspoon cayenne pepper
4   anchovies, drained, minced
6   Greek olives, minced
2   teaspoons drained capers
    Spaghetti, cooked al dente

Sauté the garlic in the olive oil in a skillet. Add the tomato, parsley and cayenne pepper. Cook until heated through. Add the anchovies, olives and capers. Cook until heated through. Toss with pasta in a serving bowl. Garnish with a sprinkling of grated Parmesan cheese.

SHRIMP AND ARTICHOKE PASTA

Serves 4 to 6

Even novice cooks will be successful with this easy dish that looks and tastes gourmet.

1   (6-ounce) jar marinated artichoke hearts
3   cloves of garlic, crushed
8   ounces fresh mushrooms, sliced
2   tablespoons olive oil
1   (8-ounce) can tomato sauce
2   (or 3) fresh tomatoes, chopped
2   teaspoons basil
1   teaspoon oregano
1   tablespoon chopped parley
1   teaspoon pepper
1¹/₂ cups cooked shrimp
8   ounces pasta, such as angel hair pasta, cooked

Drain the artichoke hearts, reserving the marinade. Sauté the garlic and mushrooms in the reserved marinade and olive oil in a skillet for 5 minutes. Add the tomato sauce, tomatoes, basil, oregano, parsley and pepper; mix well. Simmer for 10 minutes. Add the shrimp and artichokes. Cook until heated through. Serve over the pasta.

LINGUINE WITH BROCCOLI AND TOMATO

Serves 3 or 4

This is a hit with everyone from the kids to the dinner party guests.

1   (8-ounce) package linguine
1   (10-ounce) package frozen chopped broccoli
3   cloves of garlic, minced
2   tablespoons margarine
1   tomato, seeded, chopped
¹/₄ cup dry white wine or chicken broth
¹/₄ teaspoon basil
6   ounces frozen cooked shrimp, thawed

Cook the linguine and broccoli separately using the package directions; drain. Rinse the pasta with hot water and drain.

Sauté the garlic in the margarine in a large skillet until golden brown. Add the tomato, wine and basil. Simmer for 5 minutes or until the liquid is reduced to the desired consistency. Stir in the pasta, broccoli and shrimp. Cook over medium heat until heated through.

LINGUINE WITH ASPARAGUS AND MUSTARD

Serves 8

Serve hot or cold with fresh strawberries and fresh bread for a perfect spring menu.

2   pounds thin asparagus
1   (16-ounce) package linguine
1/4 cup each grainy mustard and extra-virgin olive oil
2   large shallots, thinly sliced
1   clove of garlic, minced
1½   teaspoons anchovy paste
2   tablespoons minced parsley
     Thyme to taste
2   cups chopped cooked chicken or shrimp
     Salt and pepper to taste

Slice the asparagus diagonally. Cook in a small amount of water in a saucepan for 3 minutes or until tender. Rinse with cold water and drain. Cook the pasta using the package directions; drain.

Combine the mustard, olive oil, shallots, garlic, anchovy paste, parsley and thyme in a serving bowl; mix well. Add the chicken; mix to coat well. Add the pasta and asparagus; toss gently. Season with salt and pepper.

TURKEY TAPENADE

Serves 3 or 4

Thanks to Danny Dean Beghtel, executive chef of the City Club of Rockford, for this recipe.

8   ounces turkey breast
4   ounces onion, minced
1   teaspoon minced garlic
1½   cups each broccoli flowerets, chopped zucchini and mushroom quarters
1   cup each coarsely chopped green and red bell peppers
3   ounces sun-dried tomatoes, puréed
1   tablespoon basil
½   teaspoon coarsely ground pepper
2   ounces extra-virgin olive oil
     Whipping cream
4   ounces stewed tomatoes
1   cup grated Parmesan cheese
½   teaspoon onion salt
2   cups small mostaccioli, cooked
1   cup shredded mozzarella cheese

Cut the turkey into bite-sized pieces; rinse and pat dry. Sauté the turkey with the onion, garlic, broccoli, zucchini, mushrooms, bell peppers, sun-dried tomatoes, basil and pepper in the olive oil in a large skillet over high heat for 4 to 6 minutes or until the turkey is cooked through. Reduce the heat to low. Add the cream, stewed tomatoes, Parmesan cheese and onion salt. Simmer for 4 minutes or until the cheese melts and the sauce is smooth, adding small amounts of water if needed for desired consistency. Add the pasta; mix gently. Simmer for 2 minutes. Serve topped with the mozzarella cheese.

SCALLOPS WITH TOMATO BASIL SAUCE

Serves 4

Serve this delicious sauce over capellini d'angelo (angel hair) pasta.

1 tablespoon crushed garlic
6 tablespoons olive oil
2 pounds fresh plum tomatoes, seeded, chopped
1 cup chopped fresh basil
1 teaspoon salt
1 teaspoon pepper
8 ounces bay scallops
Salt to taste
Cooked thin pasta

Sauté the garlic in the olive oil in a saucepan until tender but not brown. Add the tomatoes. Simmer to desired consistency. Add the basil, 1 teaspoon salt and pepper. Simmer for 5 minutes. Drain the scallops and sprinkle with salt to taste. Add to the saucepan. Simmer for 4 to 5 minutes or until scallops are opaque. Serve over hot pasta topped with Parmesan cheese.

CHICKEN PASTA WITH SUGAR SNAP PEAS

Serves 6

Steam the sugar snap peas for just 5 minutes, so they will retain their color and crunch for this attractive dish.

The chicken

12 ounces chicken breast filets
1 teaspoon lime juice
1 teaspoon peanut oil
2 teaspoons soy sauce
2 teaspoons chopped garlic
1 teaspoon chopped gingerroot
1/4 teaspoon hot pepper

The pasta

6 ounces sugar snap peas
1 teaspoon sesame oil
1/4 cup chopped scallions
1 teaspoon toasted sesame seeds
1/2 teaspoon salt
1 tablespoon fresh coriander
1 teaspoon fresh cilantro
12 ounces fettucini or linguine, cooked

Cut the chicken into strips; rinse and pat dry. Combine the lime juice, peanut oil, soy sauce, garlic, gingerroot and hot pepper in a bowl; mix well. Add the chicken. Let stand for 10 minutes. Sauté the chicken in the marinade in a skillet until the chicken is cooked through; drain.

Steam the peas for 5 minutes. Combine the sesame oil, scallions, sesame seeds, salt, coriander and cilantro in a large serving dish; mix well. Add the pasta, peas and chicken; toss gently to mix. Serve immediately.

PENNE AND SHRIMP QUATTRO FORMAGGIO

Serves 4

This is a specialty of Joel's Jungle Jim's Restaurant. It can also be make with grilled chicken strips or lobster.

1   pound (21 to 25-count) shrimp, peeled, deveined
1   tablespoon olive oil
1   (16-ounce) package penne
3   cups whipping cream
1/4   cup Chablis
1/2   cup grated Parmesan cheese
1/4   cup grated Romano cheese
1/3   cup shredded Gorganzola cheese
1/4   cup mascarpone cheese or additional Romano cheese
4   ounces fresh spinach
1/2   teaspoon salt
1/2   teaspoon white pepper
     Plum tomatoes

Sauté the shrimp in the olive oil in a skillet until tender; set aside. Cook the pasta using package directions for 10 to 12 minutes or until al dente; drain and keep warm.

Combine the cream and wine in a saucepan. Cook until reduced by 1/4 or until it coats a spoon. Stir in the cheeses until melted; reduce the heat. Add the spinach. Cook until wilted, stirring constantly. Season with salt and white pepper. Combine with the shrimp and pasta in a large bowl; mix gently. Garnish the servings with plum tomatoes.

DESSERTS

A house is beautiful not because of its walls,
but because of its cakes.
Old Russian Proverb

Desserts

APRICOT PRALINE CHEESECAKE

Serves 10 to 12

The crust

An updated version of a favorite dessert.

2/3 cup graham cracker crumbs
2/3 cup gingersnap crumbs
1/2 cup butter or margarine, softened
2 tablespoons sugar
1 teaspoon cinnamon
2/3 cup chopped pecans

The filling

28 ounces cream cheese, softened
1 1/2 cups packed dark brown sugar
3 tablespoons flour
4 eggs
1 1/2 teaspoons vanilla extract
1/2 cup chopped pecans

The topping

Apricot preserves
Water

Combine the cracker crumbs, cookie crumbs, butter, sugar, cinnamon and pecans in a bowl or food processor; mix well. Press into a buttered 10-inch springform pan.

Combine the cream cheese, brown sugar and flour in a mixer bowl; beat until smooth. Beat in the eggs 1 at a time. Add the vanilla and pecans; mix well. Spoon into the prepared pan. Bake at 325 degrees on the center oven rack for 1 to 1 1/2 hours or until the center is set. Cool on a wire rack. Chill for 3 hours or longer.

Thin the apricot preserves to the desired consistency with water in a small bowl. Spoon over individual cheesecake servings.

CRESCENT ROLL CHEESECAKE

Serves 6 to 8

The crescent rolls are a new idea for a delicious dessert that is easy to make and take.

2 cans crescent rolls
1 egg yolk
16 ounces cream cheese, softened
3/4 cup sugar
1 teaspoon lemon juice
1/2 teaspoon vanilla extract
1 egg white
1/4 (to 1/2) cup nuts

Unroll the crescent roll dough. Line a 9x13-inch baking dish with 1 can of the dough, pressing the edges and perforations to seal. Beat next 5 ingredients in a mixer bowl until smooth. Spread over dough. Top with the remaining dough, pressing the edges and perforations to seal.

Beat the egg white slightly with a fork in a small bowl. Brush over the dough; sprinkle with the nuts. Bake at 375 degrees for 20 to 25 minutes or until golden brown. Cool on a wire rack. Cut into squares. Store in an airtight container.

UNBELIEVABLE CARROT CAKE

Serves 24

The cake

An all-time favorite updated with several surprise additions.

2	cups flour
1	teaspoon baking soda
2	teaspoons cinnamon
1	teaspoon salt
2	cups sugar
1½	cups vegetable oil
3	eggs
2	cups grated carrots
1	cup drained crushed pineapple
1	cup coconut
1	cup chopped nuts
1	teaspoon vanilla extract

The frosting

4	ounces cream cheese, softened
¼	cup margarine, softened
1	teaspoon vanilla extract
½	(1-pound) package confectioners' sugar

Sift the flour, baking soda, cinnamon and salt together. Combine the sugar, oil and eggs in a mixer bowl; beat until thick and lemon-colored. Add the dry ingredients; mix well. Fold in the carrots, pineapple, coconut, nuts and vanilla. Spoon into a greased 9x13-inch cake pan. Bake at 350 degrees for 1 hour or until a wooden pick inserted in the center comes out clean. Cool on a wire rack.

Combine the cream cheese, margarine and vanilla in a mixer bowl; beat until light. Add the confectioners' sugar; beat until smooth. Spread over the cooled cake.

PERFECT PIE PASTRY

Serves 6 to 8

Make a perfect pie shell or double the recipe for true two-crust flaky goodness.

1 cup flour
½ teaspoon salt
⅓ cup plus 1 tablespoon shortening
2 to 3 tablespoons cold water

Combine the flour and salt in a bowl; mix well. Cut in the shortening until crumbly. Add the water 1 tablespoon at a time, mixing with a fork until dough clings together. Shape into a ball. Roll pastry 2 inches larger than inverted pie plate on lightly floured surface. Fold pastry into quarters; place in pie plate and unfold, pressing firmly against bottom and side. May substitute ⅓ cup lard for shortening. Double the recipe for a 2-crust pie.

CRUMB-TOP APPLE PIE

Serves 6 to 8

A wonderfully easy pie for the beginning cook.

The crumb topping

3/4 cup flour
1/2 cup sugar
1/3 cup margarine, softened

The pie

6 cups sliced peeled apples
1 unbaked pie shell or Pie Pastry (page 150 or 196)
1/2 cup sugar
1 teaspoon cinnamon

Combine the flour, sugar and margarine in a bowl; mix with a pastry blender or 2 knives until crumbly.

Spread the apples in the pie shell. Sprinkle with a mixture of the sugar and cinnamon. Top with the crumb mixture; press down lightly. Bake at 400 degrees for 40 to 50 minutes or until golden brown.

DUTCH APPLE PIE

Serves 8

A favorite in the fall when apples are abundant. Serve it topped with cream or ice cream.

The topping

2/3 cup sifted flour
1/3 cup packed light brown sugar
1/3 cup margarine

The pie

2 pounds tart cooking apples, peeled, thinly sliced
1 tablespoon lemon juice
3 tablespoons flour
3/4 cup sugar
1 teaspoon cinnamon
1 teaspoon allspice
Salt to taste
1 unbaked (9-inch) pie shell or Pie Pastry (page 150 or 196)

Mix the flour and brown sugar in a medium bowl. Cut in the margarine until crumbly.

Toss the apples with the lemon juice in a large bowl. Mix the flour, sugar, cinnamon, allspice and salt in a bowl. Add to the apples; toss to mix well. Spoon into the pie shell; top with the crumb mixture. Bake at 400 degrees for 45 minutes or until the apples are tender and the topping is golden brown.

SOUR CREAM APPLE PIE

Serves 6 to 8

This pie smells so good when it is cooking that it has to be served warm; it never has time to cool.

The topping

1/2	cup packed brown sugar
1/4	cup flour
1	tablespoon cinnamon
1/4	cup butter

The pie

1	egg
1/2	cup sugar
2	tablespoons flour
2	tablespoons lemon juice
1/4	teaspoon salt
1	cup sour cream
4	cups sliced peeled apples
1	unbaked deep-dish pie shell or Pie Pastry (page 150 or 196)
	Cinnamon-sugar

Combine the brown sugar, flour, cinnamon and butter in a bowl; mix until crumbly.

Combine the egg, sugar, flour, lemon juice and salt in a mixer bowl; mix well. Add the sour cream and apples; mix gently. Spoon into the pie shell. Bake at 400 degrees for 15 minutes. Reduce the oven temperature to 350 degrees. Sprinkle the topping over pie. Bake for 30 to 40 minutes or until the apples are tender and the topping is golden brown. Sprinkle with cinnamon-sugar. Serve warm.

BUTTER PECAN HEATH PIES

Serves 12 to 16

An easy and refreshing summer dessert—perfect for patio entertaining or luncheons!

The pie shells

1	cup saltine cracker crumbs
1	cup graham cracker crumbs
1/2	cup melted margarine

The filling

1/2	gallon butter pecan ice cream, softened
2	(3-ounce) packages vanilla instant pudding mix
1	cup milk
9	ounces whipped topping
4	Heath candy bars, crushed

Combine the cracker crumbs and graham cracker crumbs with the margarine in a bowl; mix well. Press into two 9-inch pie plates. Bake at 350 degrees for 10 minutes.

Combine the ice cream, pudding mix and milk in a bowl; mix until smooth. Spoon into the pie shells. Spread with a mixture of the whipped topping and candy. Freeze until serving time.

CHOCOLATE COCONUT PIE

Serves 8

The pie shell

The filling

The coconut forms the crust for this easy frozen chocolate pie.

2¹/2 cups shredded coconut
¹/4 cup butter, softened

2 (7-ounce) chocolate bars with almonds
1 large container whipped topping

Mix the coconut with the butter in a bowl. Press into a pie plate. Bake at 350 degrees for 7 minutes or until golden brown.

Melt the candy bars in a saucepan over low heat. Add to the whipped topping in a bowl; mix until smooth. Spoon into the pie shell. Freeze until serving time. Garnish the edge of the pie with whipped cream.

CHOCOLATE WALNUT PIES

Serves 12 to 16

Serve with whipped cream or whipped topping for this specialty dessert that is sure to please.

9 eggs
2¹/4 cups sugar
¹/2 cup melted margarine, cooled
¹/4 cup bourbon
2 cups corn syrup
¹/4 teaspoon salt
1 cup chocolate chips
³/4 cup chopped walnuts
2 unbaked (9-inch) pie shells or Pie Pastry (page 150 or 196)

Combine the eggs, sugar, margarine, bourbon, corn syrup and salt in a bowl; mix well. Stir in the chocolate chips and walnuts. Spoon into the pie shells. Bake at 425 degrees for 10 minutes. Reduce the oven temperature to 350 degrees. Bake for 30 to 40 minutes longer or until set. Cool on a wire rack.

ICE CREAM CRUNCH PIE

Serves 8

There is no better ice cream pie. Use both the butterscotch and fudge toppings if you can't decide on just one.

³/₄ cup rolled oats
¹/₄ cup flour
¹/₄ cup packed light brown sugar
¹/₄ cup melted butter
1 cup cashews, chopped
³/₄ cup butterscotch or fudge ice cream topping
1 butter-flavored crumb pie shell
1 quart vanilla ice cream, softened

Combine the oats, flour, brown sugar, butter and cashews in a bowl for the crunch mixture; mix well. Spread on a baking sheet. Bake at 350 degrees for 15 minutes or until golden brown. Cool on the baking sheet.

Spread ¹/₃ cup of the ice cream topping evenly over the bottom and side of the pie shell. Stir 1 cup of the crunch mixture into the ice cream in a bowl. Spread into the prepared pie shell. Freeze for 1 hour. Top with the remaining ice cream topping and crunch mixture. Freeze, covered with plastic, for 4 hours or until firm. Let stand in the refrigerator for 15 minutes before serving.

SOUR CREAM LEMON PIE

Serves 8

The tangy flavor of this pie is a refreshing change from richer desserts, especially in the summer or after a heavy meal.

1 cup sugar
3¹/₂ tablespoons cornstarch
¹/₂ cup fresh lemon juice
1 tablespoon grated lemon rind
3 egg yolks, slightly beaten
1 cup milk
¹/₄ cup butter or margarine
1 cup sour cream
1 baked (9-inch) pie shell or Pie Pastry (page 150 or 196)

Combine the sugar, cornstarch, lemon juice, lemon rind, egg yolks and milk in a saucepan. Cook over medium heat until thickened, stirring constantly. Stir in the butter. Cool to room temperature. Stir in the sour cream. Spoon into the pie shell. Chill until serving time. Garnish servings with whipped cream or whipped topping and lemon twists.

SOUR CREAM RAISIN PIE

Serves 8

This recipe has been adapted from a family recipe that predated measuring spoons.

2	tablespoons flour
1	cup sugar
1	teaspoon cinnamon
1	teaspoon nutmeg
1/2	teaspoon ground cloves
11/4	cups raisins
1	cup buttermilk
2	eggs, beaten
2	recipes Pie Pastry (page 150 or 196)

Mix the flour, sugar, cinnamon, nutmeg and cloves in a bowl. Add the raisins; toss to coat well. Add the buttermilk and eggs; mix well. Spoon into a pastry-lined deep pie plate; top with the remaining pastry. Trim the edge and cut vents. Bake at 425 degrees for 5 to 7 minutes. Reduce the oven temperature to 350 degrees. Bake for 45 to 60 minutes longer or until a knife inserted in the center comes out clean and the pastry is golden brown.

OREGON PEACH PIE

Serves 6 to 8

Make the easy no-roll pastry for this pie right in the pie plate. Serve the pie warm with vanilla ice cream. It is also good made with apples.

The topping

1/2	cup packed brown sugar
1	cup flour
1/2	cup butter, softened

The pie shell

11/2	cups flour
1	teaspoon sugar
2	tablespoons milk
1/2	cup vegetable oil
1/2	teaspoon salt

The filling

1/2	cup sugar
1/4	cup flour
2	teaspoons cinnamon
41/2	cups sliced peeled peaches

Mix the brown sugar and flour in a bowl. Add the butter; mix until crumbly.

Spray a 9-inch pie plate with nonstick cooking spray. Add the flour, sugar, milk, oil and salt; mix in the pie plate. Press over the bottom and side of the plate.

Mix the sugar, flour and cinnamon in a bowl. Add the peaches; toss to coat well. Spoon into the prepared pie plate; sprinkle with the crumb topping. Cover the edge of the pastry with foil to prevent overbrowning. Bake at 425 degrees for 35 to 40 minutes or until golden brown.

BREADS & COOKIES

Bread deals with living things, with giving life,
with growth, with the seed, the grain that nurtures.

Lionel Pollane

Breads & Cookies

CHOCOLATE CHIP COFFEE RING

Serves 12

Chocolate chips and walnuts are a delicious addition to this classic sour cream coffee cake.

The topping

1/2	cup flour
1 1/2	tablespoons baking cocoa
1/2	cup each chopped walnuts and packed brown sugar
1/4	cup butter, softened
1/2	cup chocolate chips

The coffee cake

1/2	cup butter, softened
1	cup sugar
2	eggs
2	cups flour
1	teaspoon each baking powder and baking soda
1	cup sour cream
1	teaspoon vanilla extract
1/2	cup chocolate chips

Combine the flour, cocoa, walnuts, brown sugar, butter and chocolate chips in a bowl; mix until crumbly. Set aside.

Cream the butter and sugar in a large mixer bowl until light and fluffy. Beat in the eggs. Add the flour, baking powder and baking soda; beat until smooth. Stir in the sour cream and vanilla; fold in the chocolate chips. Spoon into a greased and floured tube pan. Sprinkle with the topping. Bake at 350 degrees for 1 hour. Cool in the pan on a wire rack. Remove to a serving plate. Garnish with confectioners' sugar

PUFF PASTRY COFFEE CAKE

Serves 12

This coffee cake, from a home economics teacher with 35 years of teaching experience, is wonderful to serve for brunch or with coffee.

The coffee cake

1/2	cup margarine
1	cup flour
1	tablespoon water
1/2	cup margarine
1	cup water
1	cup flour
4	eggs
2	teaspoons almond extract

The glaze

1	cup confectioners' sugar
1	tablespoon milk

Cut 1/2 cup margarine into 1 cup flour in a bowl until crumbly. Add 1 tablespoon water; mix as for pastry. Pat into a 12-inch circle on a baking sheet. Bring 1/2 cup margarine and 1 cup water to a boil in a saucepan. Stir in 1 cup flour; remove from heat. Beat in the eggs 1 at a time. Add the almond extract; mix well. Spread over the pastry circle. Bake at 400 degrees for 45 minutes.

Glaze the coffee cake with a mixture of the confectioners' sugar and milk. Garnish with cherries and almonds.

SOUR CREAM COFFEE CAKE

Serves 8

An easy and delicious version of an old favorite.

1   cup sour cream
1/4   cup canola oil
1 1/4 cups flour
3/4   cup sugar
1/2   teaspoon baking soda
1/4   teaspoon nutmeg
1/2   teaspoon salt
       Cinnamon-sugar

Combine the sour cream, oil, flour, sugar, baking soda, nutmeg and salt in a bowl; mix well. Spoon into an 8x8-inch baking pan sprayed with vegetable cooking spray. Sprinkle with cinnamon-sugar. Bake at 350 degrees for 25 minutes or until a wooden pick inserted in the center comes out clean.

SOUR CREAM AND PECAN TEA RINGS

Serves 10 to 12

For a special Christmas treat, garnish these with cherry halves and pecans and drizzle with a buttercream frosting while still warm.

1/2   cup melted margarine
1   cup sour cream
1/2   cup sugar
1 1/2 teaspoons salt
2   envelopes dry yeast
3/4   cup warm water
1   egg, room temperature
5 1/2 (to 6 1/2) cups flour
       Melted margarine
1/2   cup packed light brown sugar
1/2   teaspoon cinnamon
1   cup chopped pecans

Combine 1/2 cup margarine, sour cream, sugar and salt in a bowl. Dissolve the yeast in the warm water in a large bowl. Add the sour cream mixture, egg and 3 cups of the flour; beat until smooth. Add enough of the remaining flour to make a stiff dough. Knead on a floured surface for 8 to 10 minutes or until smooth and elastic. Place in a greased bowl, turning to coat the surface. Let rise, covered, for 1 1/4 hours or until doubled in bulk. Punch the dough down; let rest, covered, for 15 minutes.

Divide the dough into 2 portions. Roll each portion into a 9x16-inch rectangle on a floured surface. Brush with margarine. Sprinkle with a mixture of the brown sugar, cinnamon and pecans. Roll up the dough to enclose the filling; seal the ends. Arrange each roll in a circle on a greased baking sheet; press the ends to seal. Slice 2/3 of the way through the rings at intervals; turn the slices on their sides. Let rise, covered, for 1 hour. Bake at 375 degrees for 25 minutes.

APPLE BREAD

Serves 12

This is Grandmother's tried and true recipe. You may leave out the raisins and dates if you prefer.

2/3 cup margarine, softened
2 cups sugar
2 eggs
1 cup cold coffee
3 cups flour
2 teaspoons baking soda
1/2 teaspoon nutmeg
1 teaspoon cinnamon
1/2 teaspoon salt
2 cups chopped apples
1 cup raisins
1 cup chopped dates
1 cup nuts

Combine the margarine, sugar and eggs in a mixer bowl; beat until smooth. Add the coffee; mix well. Mix the flour, baking soda, nutmeg, cinnamon and salt together. Add to the batter; mix well. Stir in the apples, raisins, dates and nuts. Spoon into 2 greased and floured loaf pans. Bake at 375 degrees for 1 hour or until a wooden pick inserted in the center comes out clean. Cool in the pans for 10 minutes; remove to a wire rack to cool completely.

BRONCO BREAD

Serves 12

Bake in muffin cups for take-along snacks and lunch boxes.

2 tablespoons butter, softened
1/4 cup hot water
1/2 cup orange juice
1 1/2 tablespoons grated orange rind
1 egg
1 cup sugar
2 cups flour
1 teaspoon baking powder
1/4 teaspoon baking soda
1/2 teaspoon salt
1 cup blueberries

Combine the butter, hot water, orange juice and orange rind in a bowl; mix well. Beat in the egg. Add the sugar, flour, baking powder, baking soda and salt; mix just until moistened. Fold in the blueberries. Spoon into a greased 5x9-inch loaf pan. Bake at 325 degrees for 1 hour and 10 minutes or until a wooden pick inserted in the center comes out clean. Remove to a wire rack to cool.

LEMON BREAD

Serves 12

The tangy taste of this bread will please those who fancy the flavor of lemon.

6   tablespoons butter, softened
1   cup sugar
2   eggs
1/2   cup milk
      Grated rind of 1 lemon
1 1/2 cups flour
2   teaspoons baking powder
1/2   teaspoon salt
      Juice of 1 lemon
1/2   cup sugar

Combine the butter, 1 cup sugar and eggs in a mixer bowl; beat until smooth. Add the milk; mix by hand. Stir in the lemon rind. Sift the flour, baking powder and salt together. Add to the batter; mix well. Spoon into an ungreased 5x9-inch loaf pan. Bake at 350 degrees for 45 minutes. Cool in the pan for 10 minutes; remove to a wire rack. Drizzle with a mixture of the lemon juice and 1/2 cup sugar.

CHEDDAR CHEESE POPOVERS

Serves 12

Children love these. They are especially good with hearty fall and winter soups and stews.

2   eggs
1   cup water
1   cup flour
1/2   teaspoon salt
1/4   cup packed shredded sharp Cheddar cheese

Combine the eggs, water, flour and salt in a bowl; whisk until smooth. Add the cheese; mix well. Fill greased muffin cups 2/3 full. Bake at 425 degrees for 15 minutes. Reduce the oven temperature to 350 degrees. Bake for 35 minutes longer. Remove from the muffin cups and pierce each popover to allow steam to escape and ensure crispness. May keep warm in a warm oven for up to 10 minutes.

SCONES

Serves 12

Treat your friends and family to this version of the classic English treat.

2½ cups flour
¼ cup sugar
2 teaspoons baking powder
½ teaspoon baking soda
½ teaspoon salt
¾ cup butter
½ cup buttermilk
1 egg
½ cup currants or raisins

Mix the flour, sugar, baking powder, baking soda and salt in a bowl. Cut in the butter with a pastry cutter or 2 knives until crumbly. Add a mixture of ½ cup buttermilk and egg; toss lightly with a fork to mix well. Add the currants; mix well. Knead 5 or 6 times on a lightly floured surface. Pat into a circle ½ inch thick. Cut into rounds with 2-inch biscuit cutter; arrange on a lightly buttered baking sheet. Brush the tops with additional buttermilk. Bake at 450 degrees for 10 to 12 minutes or until golden brown.

POPPY SEED WAFFLES

Serves 6 to 8

Serve these light waffles with fresh fruit and confectioners' sugar or fruited syrups for a special occasion.

2 cups flour
⅓ cup sugar
1 tablespoon baking powder
1 tablespoon poppy seeds
1 teaspoon salt
2 egg whites
2 egg yolks, beaten
½ cup melted butter
¼ cup vegetable oil
1¾ cups milk
1 teaspoon vanilla extract
½ teaspoon almond extract

Mix the flour, sugar, baking powder, poppy seeds and salt in a medium bowl. Beat the egg whites in a mixer bowl until soft peaks form. Add the dry ingredients, egg yolks, butter, oil, milk and flavorings; mix just until moistened. Pour 1 cup at a time into heated waffle iron. Bake using manufacturer's directions.

APPLE AND RAISIN MUFFINS

Serves 12

Whip these up in a jiffy when you have some spare time and freeze them for breakfast, brunch and snacks.

- ³/₄ cup vegetable oil
- 1 cup sugar
- 2 eggs
- 1 teaspoon vanilla extract
- 2 cups flour
- ³/₄ teaspoon baking soda
- ³/₄ teaspoon cinnamon
- ¹/₂ teaspoon salt
- 1¹/₂ cups chopped apples
- ¹/₂ cup raisins
- ¹/₂ cup chopped walnuts

Combine the oil and sugar in a mixer bowl; beat for 2 minutes. Add the eggs and vanilla; beat for 1 minute. Mix the flour, baking soda, cinnamon and salt together. Add to the batter; mix just until moistened. Stir in the apples, raisins and walnuts. Spoon into greased muffin cups. Bake at 400 degrees for 15 to 20 minutes. Cool in the pans for 5 minutes; remove to a wire rack to cool completely.

TRI-BERRY MUFFINS

Serves 20

Select the berries your family likes best or use all of one kind if you prefer.

- 3 cups flour
- 1 tablespoon baking powder
- ¹/₂ teaspoon baking soda
- 4 teaspoons cinnamon
- ¹/₂ teaspoon salt
- 1¹/₄ cups milk
- 2 large eggs
- 1 cup melted butter or margarine
- 1 cup blueberries
- ¹/₂ cup sliced strawberries
- ¹/₂ cup raspberries
- 1¹/₂ cups sugar

Mix the flour, baking powder, baking soda, cinnamon and salt in a large bowl; make a well in the center. Add the milk, eggs and butter to the well; mix just until moistened. Stir in the berries and sugar. Spoon into paper-lined muffin cups, filling almost to the top. Bake at 375 degrees for 20 minutes or until brown and crusty. Remove to a wire rack to cool.

FUDGE MUFFINS

Serves 12

What could be better than a wonderful muffin with a rich fudgy taste sure to please every sweet tooth?

1 cup margarine
2 (1-ounce) squares baking chocolate
2 cups sugar
1½ cups flour
4 eggs
1½ teaspoons vanilla extract
½ teaspoon salt
1 cup chopped nuts (optional)

Melt the margarine and chocolate in a 1-quart saucepan, stirring to blend well; remove from the heat. Add the sugar, flour, eggs, vanilla and salt; mix well. Stir in the nuts. Spoon into greased muffin cups. Bake at 325 degrees for 25 to 30 minutes or until a wooden pick inserted in the center comes out clean; do not overbake. Remove immediately to a wire rack to cool.

OATMEAL AND RAISIN MUFFINS

Serves 15 to 18

Wonderful—a unique, delicious and moist special muffin!

1 cup raisins
½ cup sherry
2 cups flour
1 cup rolled oats
1 cup packed brown sugar
1 tablespoon baking powder
1 teaspoon salt
2 eggs
¾ cup buttermilk
½ cup vegetable oil
1 teaspoon vanilla extract
½ tablespoon cinnamon
1 cup chopped pecans
½ cup sugar
1 tablespoon cinnamon

Mix the raisins with the wine in a small bowl; let stand for 15 minutes.

Combine the flour, oats, brown sugar, baking powder and salt in a large mixer bowl. Add the eggs, buttermilk, oil, vanilla and ½ tablespoon cinnamon; mix well. Stir in the raisin mixture and pecans. Spoon into greased muffin cups, filling ⅔ full. Sprinkle with a mixture of sugar and 1 tablespoon cinnamon. Bake at 375 degrees for 20 to 23 minutes or until a wooden pick inserted in the center comes out clean. Remove to a wire rack to cool.

SPICE MUFFINS

Serves 24

A low-fat muffin recipe that is just as good baked in a bundt pan; increase the baking time to 50 to 60 minutes.

2³/4 cups flour
2¹/4 cups sugar
2¹/2 teaspoons baking soda
1¹/4 teaspoons baking powder
1   teaspoon cinnamon
¹/2   teaspoon allspice
¹/2   teaspoon salt
¹/4   teaspoon cloves
1³/4 cups applesauce
1¹/4 cups vanilla yogurt
2   eggs
¹/3   cup vegetable oil
1   cup raisins (optional)
1   cup nuts (optional)

Mix the flour, sugar, baking soda, baking powder, cinnamon, allspice, salt and cloves in a large bowl. Add the applesauce, yogurt, eggs and oil; mix well. Stir in the raisins and nuts. Spoon into greased muffin cups. Bake at 350 degrees for 20 minutes or until a wooden pick inserted in the center comes out clean. Remove to a wire rack to cool.

MAMA TARABORI'S BISCOTTI

Yields 24

This will satisfy most American tastes for a real Italian treat. For a more traditional version, place the slices on a baking sheet and toast in a 350-degree oven for 10 minutes on each side.

¹/2   cup butter, softened
1   cup sugar
3   eggs
2   cups plus 2 tablespoons sifted flour
2¹/4 teaspoons baking powder
2   teaspoons anise extract
2   tablespoons anise seeds
1   package whole almonds

Cream the butter and sugar in a mixer bowl until light and fluffy. Beat in the eggs 1 at a time. Add a mixture of the flour and baking powder gradually, mixing until smooth. Add the anise extract and anise seeds; mix well. Fold in the almonds. Spoon onto a greased and floured baking sheet; shape into a rectangle 2 inches wide. Bake at 350 degrees for 15 to 20 minutes or until golden brown. Remove to a cutting board; slice diagonally while still warm.

TURTLE BROWNIES

Yields 18

A golden oldie that is still a favorite with young and old alike.

1   cup margarine
1/2 cup baking cocoa
1 3/4 cups sugar
1   cup flour
1   teaspoon vanilla extract
2   eggs
1   (14-ounce) package caramels
1/3 cup evaporated milk
1 1/2 cups pecan pieces

Melt the margarine in a saucepan. Blend in the cocoa. Add the sugar, flour and vanilla; mix well. Beat in the eggs. Spoon half the batter into a greased and floured 9x13-inch baking pan. Bake at 350 degrees for 10 minutes.

Melt the caramels with the evaporated milk in a saucepan, stirring to blend well. Spoon over the baked layer. Spoon the remaining batter over the caramel layer; sprinkle with the pecans. Bake for 10 to 15 minutes longer or until the brownies pull from side of pan. Cool on a wire rack. Cut into squares.

CRISPY CEREAL NUT COOKIES

Yields 96

A great cookie for children! They can help with shaping and pressing with the fork—and, of course, with the eating.

1/2 cup butter, softened
1/2 cup sugar
1/2 cup packed brown sugar
1   egg
1/2 cup vegetable oil
1/2 tablespoon buttermilk
1 3/4 cups flour
1/2 teaspoon baking soda
1/2 teaspoon salt
3/4 teaspoon vanilla extract
1/2 cup corn flakes
1/2 cup quick-cooking oats
1/4 cup coconut
1/2 cup chopped nuts

Cream the butter, sugar and brown sugar in a mixer bowl until light and fluffy. Add the egg, oil and buttermilk; mix well. Sift in the flour, baking soda and salt; mix well. Stir in the vanilla, corn flakes, oats, coconut and nuts. Chill in the refrigerator. Shape by teaspoonfuls into balls. Place on a cookie sheet; press with a fork to flatten. Bake at 350 degrees for 8 to 10 minutes or until golden brown. Remove the cookies to a wire rack to cool.

ITALIAN CHOCOLATE COOKIES

Yields 200 to 250

The cookies

Grandmother's recipe for special occasions.

2 cups shortening
1 (8-ounce) can baking cocoa
3 cups sugar
2 cups milk
6 eggs
Juice of 1 lemon
10 cups flour
3 tablespoons baking powder
1 teaspoon cinnamon
1 teaspoon allspice
1 teaspoon salt
1/2 (15-ounce) package raisins
1 cup chopped nuts
Chocolate chips (optional)

The frosting

1 (1-pound) package confectioners' sugar
1 tablespoon vanilla extract
Milk

Melt the shortening in a saucepan. Blend in the cocoa, sugar and 2 cups milk. Add the eggs and lemon juice; mix well. Sift in the flour, baking powder, cinnamon, allspice and salt; mix well. Add the raisins, nuts and chocolate chips; mix well with hands if necessary. Shape into small balls; place on oiled cookie sheet. Bake at 400 degrees on lower oven rack for 5 minutes. Move the cookie sheet to the upper oven rack. Bake for 5 minutes longer. Remove to a wire rack to cool.

Mix the confectioners' sugar and vanilla with enough milk to make of spreading consistency. Spread on the cooled cookies.

LEMON COOKIES

Yields 30

Great-Grandmother's 100-year-old recipe.

2 eggs
2/3 cup vegetable oil
2 teaspoons vanilla extract
2 teaspoons grated lemon rind
3/4 cup sugar
2 cups flour
2 teaspoons baking powder
1/2 teaspoon salt

Beat the eggs with a fork in a bowl until smooth. Stir in the oil, vanilla and lemon rind. Add 3/4 cup sugar; beat until thick. Sift in the flour, baking powder and salt; mix well. Drop by teaspoonfuls 2 inches apart on a cookie sheet. Press with the bottom of a glass dipped in additional sugar. Bake at 350 degrees for 6 to 8 minutes or until golden brown. Remove immediately to a wire rack to cool.

MARSHMALLOW AND NUT BARS

Yields 36

Everyone in the family will love these crunchy bars.

The baked layer

1½ cups flour
2/3 cup packed brown sugar
½ teaspoon baking powder
¼ teaspoon baking soda
½ teaspoon salt
½ cup margarine, softened
1 teaspoon vanilla extract
2 egg yolks
3 cups miniature marshmallows

The topping

2/3 cup white corn syrup
¼ cup margarine
2 cups peanut butter chips
2 teaspoons vanilla extract
2 cups crisp rice cereal
2 cups cocktail peanuts

Mix the flour, brown sugar, baking powder, baking soda and salt in a bowl. Add the margarine, vanilla and egg yolks; mix well. Press into an ungreased 9x13-inch baking pan. Bake at 350 degrees for 12 to 15 minutes or until light brown. Sprinkle immediately with the marshmallows. Bake for 1 to 2 minutes longer or until the marshmallows begin to puff. Cool on a wire rack.

Combine the corn syrup, margarine, peanut butter chips and vanilla in a saucepan. Cook over medium heat until the margarine and chips melt, stirring to blend well; remove from the heat. Stir in the cereal and peanuts. Spread evenly over the baked layer. Chill until serving time. Cut into bars.

MINT MERINGUE PUFFS

Yields 36

These are so easy, but they have the smooth and rich taste of a very expensive sweet.

2 egg whites
½ teaspoon cream of tartar
Salt to taste
3/4 cup sugar
1 (or 2) drops of green food coloring
10 ounces mint chips

Combine the egg whites, cream of tartar and salt in a mixer bowl; beat until foamy. Add the sugar gradually, beating constantly until stiff and glossy. Fold in the food coloring and mint chips. Drop by teaspoonfuls onto cookie sheet lined with waxed paper. Place in a 375-degree oven; turn off the oven. Let stand in the oven with door closed for 2 hours to overnight. Store in an airtight container.

A DIFFERENT OATMEAL COOKIE

Yields 36 to 48

The name says it all! These delicate cookies are pastry-like or tart-like in texture, similar to Swedish cookies.

1/2 cup butter, softened
1/2 cup margarine, softened
1/2 cup sugar
1 cup flour
1 1/2 cups quick-cooking oats
1 teaspoon vanilla extract
Confectioners' sugar

Cream the butter, margarine and sugar in a mixer bowl until light and fluffy. Add the flour, oats and vanilla; mix well. Shape into small balls. Drop into a bowl of confectioners' sugar, turning to coat well. Place on ungreased cookie sheet; press with bottom of glass dipped in additional confectioners' sugar or flour. Bake at 350 degrees for 8 minutes. Cool on cookie sheet for 2 minutes. Remove carefully with spatula to waxed paper to cool completely. Sift additional confectioners' sugar over cookies.

OATMEAL CARMELITAS

Yields 16

Rich and tasty, but easy to do!

1 (14-ounce) package caramels
5 tablespoons whipping cream or evaporated milk
1 cup flour
1 cup rolled oats
1/2 teaspoon baking soda
3/4 cup packed brown sugar
1/4 teaspoon salt
1/2 cup melted butter
1 cup chocolate chips
1/2 cup chopped pecans

Melt the caramels with the cream in a double boiler over hot water, stirring to blend well. Mix the flour, oats, baking soda, brown sugar, salt and melted butter in a bowl until crumbly. Press half the mixture into an 8x8-inch baking pan. Bake at 350 degrees for 10 minutes. Sprinkle with the chocolate chips and pecans. Spread with the caramel mixture. Crumble the remaining oats mixture over the top. Bake for 15 minutes longer. Cool on a wire rack for 2 hours. Cut into bars.

SCOTCH SHORTBREAD COOKIES

Yields 36

Without the chocolate candy and the pecans, this is a Scottish shortbread. It is wonderful either way. Do not substitute margarine or shortening for the butter.

1   cup butter, softened
1/2   cup packed brown sugar
2 1/2 cups sifted flour
       Chocolate bars
       Pecans

Combine the butter, brown sugar and flour in a bowl; mix well. Shape into balls. Place on a cookie sheet; press in a crisscross pattern with a fork to flatten. Bake at 300 degrees for 20 to 25 minutes or until golden brown.

Melt the chocolate bars in a double boiler over hot water. Spread over the cookies; sprinkle with the pecans.

PECAN BRITTLE SNACK

Yields 48

This doubly delicious snack doubles as a candy or a cookie.

48   rectangular club crackers
1   cup butter
1/2   cup sugar
3/4   cup chopped pecans

Line a 10x15-inch baking pan with foil. Arrange the crackers in the pan in 8 rows of 6 crackers. Melt the butter with the sugar in a saucepan, stirring to mix well. Boil for 2 minutes, stirring frequently. Cool slightly. Pour over the crackers; sprinkle with the pecans. Bake at 325 degrees for 15 minutes. Remove immediately to waxed paper to cool. Store in airtight container.

RUM BALLS

Yields 24

A traditional favorite for the holidays.

2   tablespoons baking cocoa
2   cups confectioners' sugar
1/4 cup rum, bourbon or brandy
2   tablespoons white corn syrup
2   cups finely crushed vanilla wafers
1   cup finely chopped walnuts
2   tablespoons confectioners' sugar

Mix the cocoa and 1 cup of the confectioners' sugar in a medium bowl. Add 1 cup confectioners' sugar, rum, corn syrup, cookie crumbs and walnuts in the order listed, mixing well after each addition. Shape into 1 1/4-inch balls. Roll in 2 tablespoons confectioners' sugar. Let stand overnight. Store in an airtight container.

RUM TRUFFLES

Yields 36

The perfect Christmas gift for hostesses!

2   (1-ounce) squares unsweetened chocolate, shaved
2   cups semisweet chocolate chips
1   cup melted butter
4   teaspoons rum
2   teaspoons vanilla extract
2/3 cup crushed gingersnaps
2/3 cup baking cocoa
2/3 cup instant coffee granules

Combine the unsweetened chocolate and chocolate chips in a microwave-safe dish. Microwave on High for 3 to 5 minutes or until melted; mix well. Add the butter, rum and vanilla; mix well. Stir in the cookie crumbs. Chill for 1 1/2 to 2 hours.

Shape the chilled mixture into balls. Roll in a mixture of the cocoa and coffee granules. Store in an airtight container.

TURTLES

Yields 48

A delicious dessert or hostess gift any time of the year.

1   (10-ounce) package pecan halves
1   (14-ounce) package caramels
1   tablespoon butter
2   tablespoons evaporated milk
2   cups chocolate chips

Arrange the pecan halves by threes so the tips meet in a clover pattern on a buttered tray. Melt the caramels and butter with the evaporated milk in a saucepan, stirring to blend well. Spoon over the pecans. Chill for 30 minutes or longer. Melt the chocolate chips in a double boiler over hot water. Spoon over the caramel mixture. Let stand until firm. Store in the refrigerator.

PEOPLE PUPPY CHOW

Serves 20

You won't be able to keep your chow hounds out of the puppy chow.

1   cup peanut butter
1   cup chocolate chips
1/2   cup butter
10   cups Crispix cereal
3   cups confectioners' sugar

Melt the peanut butter with the chocolate chips and butter in a saucepan, stirring to blend well. Pour over the cereal in a large bowl; toss to coat well. Combine with the confectioners' sugar in a large food storage bag; shake to coat well. Store in an airtight container.

That Extra Touch

FRENCH DRESSING

Serves 16

Grandmother's tried-and-true salad dressing recipe.

1	clove of garlic, minced
1	cup sugar
1/3	cup vinegar
1	teaspoon Worcestershire sauce
1	small onion, grated
2/3	cup catsup
1	teaspoon salt
2	cups salad oil

Combine the garlic, sugar, vinegar, Worcestershire sauce, onion, catsup and salt in a bowl. Beat with a rotary beater until smooth. Add the oil gradually, beating until smooth. Store in the refrigerator.

EASY HOMEMADE MAYONNAISE

Serves 12

You can vary this easy recipe to suit your tastes and the occasion. Try a different oil, such as olive oil or canola oil, for all or part of the corn oil; use a different mustard; substitute orange juice or a vinegar such as wine vinegar or tarragon vinegar for the lemon juice; or add your own special touches.

2	large eggs
1	tablespoon fresh lemon juice
1/4	teaspoon sugar
2	teaspoons Dijon mustard
1/2	teaspoon salt
1/8	teaspoon white pepper
1 1/2	cups corn oil

Combine the eggs, lemon juice, sugar, mustard, salt and white pepper in a blender container; process for several seconds or until well mixed. Add the oil very gradually, processing constantly until the mixture thickens and scraping the sides of the container after the mixture begins to thicken. Chill until serving time. Correct the seasonings. Store in the refrigerator.

GARLIC AND MUSTARD DRESSING

Serves 20

This is also good as a condiment with pot roast.

1   egg
1/3   cup Dijon mustard
2/3   cup red wine vinegar
      Salt and pepper to taste
3   cloves of garlic, chopped
4   tablespoons minced red onion
2   cups olive oil

Combine the egg, mustard, vinegar, salt and pepper in a food processor container fitted with a steel blade; process for 1 minute. Add the garlic and onion, processing constantly. Add the olive oil very gradually; process constantly until smooth. Correct the seasonings. Store in the refrigerator.

GREEK VINAIGRETTE

Serves 4 to 6

An authentic dressing to use on a Greek salad.

1/3   cup olive oil
3   tablespoons wine vinegar
2   tablespoons lemon juice
1½   teaspoons chopped fresh or dried oregano
1   teaspoon sugar
1   small clove of garlic, minced
1/4   teaspoon pepper

Combine the olive oil, vinegar, lemon juice, oregano, sugar, garlic and pepper in a covered jar. Shake to mix well. Store in the refrigerator for up to 2 weeks. Shake the mixture before serving.

HERB-FLAVORED VINEGAR

Serves variable number

Flavored vinegars make wonderful gifts; add a note suggesting they be added in salad dressings and mayonnaise or in pickles and sauces. They are a good way to use the bounty of your herb harvest at its peak.

4   herbs such as thyme, parsley, rosemary, sage or scallions/chives
1/4 teaspoon minced garlic
1/2 teaspoon peppercorns
     Wine vinegar or cider vinegar

Place the herbs, garlic and peppercorns in sterilized jars. Fill the jars with the vinegar; seal tightly. Let stand for 2 weeks. Strain the vinegar into decorative jars; add a fresh sprig of tarragon or 1 of the herbs. Seal the jars.

RASPBERRY VINAIGRETTE

Serves 10 to 16

Serve this on a salad of mixed greens. It is also good on warmed Brie as an appetizer.

1   cup olive oil
1   cup corn oil
1/4 cup raspberry spreadable fruit
2/3 cup raspberry vinegar
     Salt and pepper to taste
2   (to 4) tablespoons chopped shallots (optional)
2   (to 4) tablespoons chopped parsley (optional)

Combine the olive oil, corn oil, spreadable fruit, vinegar, salt and pepper in a bowl; mix well. Add the shallots and parsley; mix well. Store in the refrigerator.

ALL-PURPOSE BASTING SAUCE

Serves 6

This makes enough basting sauce to baste three pounds of chicken, pork, beef or fish for broiling, baking or grilling. It can also be used for grilling vegetables.

1/2   cup vegetable oil
1/2   cup lemon juice
1/2   cup wine vinegar
1/4   cup soy sauce
       Salt and pepper to taste

Combine the oil, lemon juice, vinegar, soy sauce, salt and pepper in a covered jar; shake to mix well. Store in the refrigerator.

MARINADE AND BASTING SAUCE

Serves 10 to 12

A southern recipe, this sauce can be used to marinate three pounds of beef, chicken or ribs before grilling. Reserve the marinade and brush it on as a basting sauce toward the end of the grilling time.

1/2   cup white vinegar
1   cup water
2   tablespoons Worcestershire sauce
1/4   cup vegetable oil
1   clove of garlic, minced
2   teaspoons salt
1   teaspoon pepper

Combine the vinegar, water, Worcestershire sauce, oil, garlic, salt and pepper in a saucepan. Bring to a boil. Use as marinade and basting sauce.

BARBECUE SAUCE

Serves 12

An easy and tasty sauce for barbecuing chicken, chops or ribs.

3/4   cup catsup
3/4   cup water
2   tablespoons brown sugar
2   tablespoons vinegar
2   tablespoons Worcestershire sauce
1   onion, chopped
1   teaspoon paprika
1   teaspoon chili powder
3/4   teaspoon pepper

Combine the catsup, water, brown sugar, vinegar, Worcestershire sauce, onion, paprika, chili powder and pepper in a bowl; mix well.

SAUCE BEARNAISE BASE

Serves 6

Delicious served with beef filets or salmon steaks or as a dip for beef fondue.

3   tablespoons wine vinegar
1   tablespoon water
1   teaspoon tarragon
2   teaspoons minced green onion tops
2   teaspoons minced parsley
     Salt and pepper to taste
3   egg yolks
3/4   cup melted butter

Combine the vinegar, water, tarragon, green onion tops, parsley, salt and pepper in a small saucepan. Cook over low heat until reduced to a glaze and most of the liquid is evaporated. Now make Easy Hollandaise Sauce (page 182) in same saucepan with cooled glaze.

COYOTE SAUCE

Serves 12

A spicy sauce for cooking chicken or pork in the oven or on the grill.

1/3   cup cider vinegar
1/3   cup vegetable oil
1   cup catsup
1/3   cup Worcestershire sauce
1/2   cup packed brown sugar
3   (or 4) cloves of garlic, minced
1   teaspoon Tabasco sauce or to taste
2   teaspoons dry mustard
1   bay leaf
1/2   teaspoon salt
1/2   teaspoon pepper

Combine the vinegar, oil, catsup, Worcestershire sauce, brown sugar, garlic, Tabasco sauce, dry mustard, bay leaf, salt and pepper in a medium saucepan. Simmer for 30 minutes, stirring frequently; remove the bay leaf before using.

EASY HOLLANDAISE SAUCE

Serves 6

A great sauce for vegetables and Eggs Benedict.

2   large egg yolks
3   tablespoons lemon juice
1/2   cup butter, chilled

Combine the egg yolks and lemon juice in a small saucepan. Add half the butter in 1 piece. Cook over low heat until the butter melts, stirring constantly. Add the remaining butter. Cook until the butter melts and the sauce is thickened to the desired consistency, stirring constantly.

GARLIC CONFIT

Serves 16

Serve garlic confit on warm French bread for a taste treat. Also good as a condiment to beef, pork, and chicken entrées. Reserve the olive oil in which the garlic is cooked and store to use in a vinaigrette.

1 cup large cloves of garlic
1 cup (about) extra-virgin olive oil

Combine the garlic with olive oil to cover in a small saucepan. Simmer over medium-low heat for 20 minutes or until the garlic is tender. Use the garlic immediately or store it covered with the olive oil in a covered jar in the refrigerator. To warm chilled garlic confit, remove it from the oil and reheat it in a sauté pan over low heat.

MARINADE FOR SIRLOIN STEAK

Serves 6

Just as good on ham steaks!

1/2 cup soy sauce
1/2 cup vegetable oil
1/2 cup packed brown sugar
2 (or 3) cloves of garlic, chopped
1/2 teaspoon ginger

Combine the soy sauce, oil, brown sugar, garlic and ginger in a blender container; process until smooth. Marinate 1 1/2-inch to 2 1/2-inch thick steaks in a sealed food storage bag in the refrigerator for 6 hours or longer.

STEAK MARINADE

Serves 4 to 6

A spicy marinade for grilling steaks or shish kabob.

1   cup soy sauce
2   tablespoons vegetable oil
2   tablespoons sesame oil
1   cup sugar
1   tablespoon minced garlic
1   tablespoon shredded ginger
1/2   teaspoon cayenne pepper
1/2   teaspoon black pepper

Combine the soy sauce with the vegetable oil, sesame oil, sugar, garlic, ginger, cayenne pepper and black pepper in a shallow dish; mix well. Use to marinate steak in the refrigerator overnight.

BEEF MARINADE

Serves 8

The mustard gives this marinade a different flavor. Use it to marinate steaks for the grill. It is also good for marinating shish kabobs made by alternating cubes of sirloin steak with cherry tomatoes, mushrooms, onions and zucchini on skewers.

1   cup vegetable oil
3/4   cup soy sauce
1/2   cup lemon juice
1/4   cup Worcestershire sauce
1/4   cup prepared mustard
2   cloves of garlic, minced
1   teaspoon pepper

Combine the oil, soy sauce, lemon juice, Worcestershire sauce, mustard, garlic and pepper in a shallow dish; mix well.

MUSTARD DILL SAUCE

Serves 4

A good sauce to serve over fish or chicken.

1   cup sliced mushrooms
1/4 cup chopped onion
1   tablespoon butter
2/3 cup milk
1/3 cup sour cream
1   tablespoon flour
1   teaspoon Dijon mustard
1/2 teaspoon dillweed
1/2 teaspoon salt
1/4 teaspoon pepper

Sauté the mushrooms and onion in the butter in a saucepan. Add the milk, sour cream, flour, mustard, dillweed, salt and pepper. Cook until thickened to desired consistency, stirring constantly.

SPICY MUSTARD

Serves 8

Make this German recipe in quantities to give in decorative jars. Its spicy flavor is good in small quantities with cheese, meats and poultry or in sauces and salad dressings.

1/4 cup white mustard seeds
1/2 cup white wine vinegar
1/2 teaspoon grated horseradish
1/2 teaspoon nutmeg
1/4 teaspoon allspice
     Salt and pepper to taste

Crush the mustard seeds in a coffee grinder or blender. Combine with the vinegar, horseradish, nutmeg and allspice in a small saucepan; mix well. Cook for 5 minutes or until thickened, stirring constantly. Season with salt and pepper. Spoon into sterilized jars; seal with 2-piece lids. Store for at least 1 week to mature before using.

HOMEMADE MUSTARD

Serves 50

This is a favorite dipping sauce with pretzels for the sports-watching crowd. Store any leftovers in the refrigerator and reheat them, if desired, in a saucepan or microwave.

1/2   cup dry mustard
1   cup white vinegar
3   eggs
1   cup packed brown sugar
1   tablespoon flour
1   beef bouillon cube

Combine the dry mustard, vinegar, eggs, brown sugar, flour and bouillon cube in a blender container; process until smooth. Cook in a saucepan until thickened to desired consistency, stirring constantly. Serve warm or chilled.

CHAMPAGNE MUSHROOM SAUCE

Serves 4

A wonderful sauce for light seafood such as sole.

1   cup sliced mushrooms
1/4   cup chopped onion
1   tablespoon butter
1   tablespoon flour
1/4   teaspoon salt
1/8   teaspoon pepper
1/2   cup milk
1/3   cup sour cream
1/3   cup dry Champagne

Sauté the mushrooms and onion in the butter in a saucepan. Stir in the flour, salt and pepper. Add the milk, sour cream and Champagne. Cook the sauce until thickened, stirring constantly.

PESTO GENOVESE

Serves 4

An old family recipe that makes enough pesto to toss with one pound of cooked pasta. Serve with Parmesan cheese.

2   cloves of garlic, crushed
1¹/₂ cups packed fresh basil leaves
¹/₂ cup packed fresh parsley leaves
2   tablespoons pine nuts
¹/₃ cup vegetable oil
¹/₂ cup grated Parmesan cheese

Combine the garlic, basil, parsley, pine nuts, oil and cheese in a blender; process until smooth. Store, covered, in the refrigerator.

BASIL AND TOMATO SAUCE

Serves 8

A low-calorie Marinara sauce, this can be served over cooked angel hair pasta, scallops, shrimp or broiled chicken; garnish with Parmesan cheese.

3   (to 5) cloves of garlic, minced
¹/₄ cup olive oil
2   (28-ounce) cans tomatoes, crushed
1   (6-ounce) can tomato paste
¹/₄ (to ¹/₂) cup chopped fresh basil leaves
    Freshly ground pepper to taste

Sauté the garlic in the olive oil in a large saucepan. Add the tomatoes and tomato paste; mix well. Cook over medium heat for 20 to 30 minutes or until of desired consistency. Add the basil and pepper. Simmer for several minutes longer.

CREAMY TOMATO SAUCE FOR PASTA

Serves 4 to 6

This pasta sauce has an outstanding flavor; add fresh mushrooms, zucchini or other vegetables of your choice for a primavera sauce.

1	large sweet onion, chopped
3	tablespoons olive oil
1	cup chopped tomatoes
1/2	cup beef broth
1/4	cup white wine
1/4	cup grated Parmesan cheese
1	tablespoon chopped fresh basil or 1 teaspoon dried basil
2	tablespoons chopped fresh parsley
1	cup whipping cream
	Salt and pepper to taste

Sauté the onion in the olive oil in a saucepan. Add the tomatoes. Cook for 5 minutes. Add the beef broth, wine, cheese, basil and parsley. Cook until heated through. Stir in the cream, salt and pepper. Cook just until the mixture begins to boil and sauce is reduced to desired consistency.

VEGETABLE MARINARA SAUCE

Serves 6 to 8

For a nice Lenten dinner, serve this over cheese-filled ravioli or other pasta along with an Italian salad and garlic bread with olive oil.

1	large onion, chopped
8	ounces mushrooms, sliced
1	large green bell pepper, chopped
1	large red bell pepper, chopped
1	small zucchini, chopped
1	(12-ounce) can stewed tomatoes
4	(8-ounce) cans tomato sauce
2	(6-ounce) cans tomato paste
2	cloves of garlic, crushed
1	cup water
1	tablespoon basil
1	teaspoon oregano
1/2	teaspoon pepper

Combine the onion, mushrooms, green bell pepper, red bell pepper, zucchini, tomatoes, tomato sauce, tomato paste, garlic, water, basil, oregano and pepper in a slow cooker; mix well. Cook on Low for 8 to 9 hours or on High for 4 to 5 hours or until of the desired consistency.

BRANDIED CRUMB CRUST FOR TURKEY

Serves 20

This is one innovation for your Thanksgiving turkey that your family will want to welcome as a tradition for years to come. It makes enough to cover an eighteen-pound to twenty-pound turkey.

7   cloves of garlic, minced
1½ pounds unsalted butter, softened
5   cups coarse stale bread crumbs
5   tablespoons Cognac or brandy

Combine the garlic and butter in a bowl; mix well. Stir in the bread crumbs with a large spoon. Add the Cognac. Spread the mixture evenly over the turkey with floured hands, covering completely. Roast as usual.

BOURBON GLAZE FOR HAM

Serves 16

Great for your holiday ham or summer cookouts!

¾   cup bourbon
1   cup packed brown sugar
3   cups water
12 whole cloves

Combine the bourbon, brown sugar, water and cloves in a saucepan. Cook over low heat until the brown sugar dissolves, stirring frequently. Brush over the ham 3 or 4 times during the last 15 minutes of cooking time.

HOMEMADE CAJUN SEASONING

Serves many

A spicy seasoning for chicken, fish, pork or shrimp.

1/2	cup paprika
2	tablespoons garlic powder
1 1/2	tablespoons salt
1	tablespoon cayenne pepper
1	tablespoon thyme
1	tablespoon basil
1	tablespoon oregano
1 1/2	teaspoons poultry seasoning
1 1/2	teaspoons each white pepper and black pepper

Combine the paprika, garlic powder, salt, cayenne pepper, thyme, basil, oregano, poultry seasoning, white pepper and black pepper in a small bowl; mix well. Store in an airtight container.

HERBES DE PROVENCE

Serves many

This fragrant herb mixture is used liberally in all French cooking from pork terrine to grilled meat marinades to green salads and vinaigrettes.

3	tablespoons (heaping) thyme
1 1/2	tablespoons (heaping) oregano
1 1/2	tablespoons (heaping) summer savory
3	tablespoons (heaping) marjoram

Combine the thyme, oregano, savory and marjoram in a covered jar; mix well. Store in a dark place.

CRANBERRY CHUTNEY

Serves 16

Serve with a succulent glazed ham for a special holiday or buffet dinner. Also good with pork and turkey.

1¹/3 cups boiling water
1   cup raisins
2   cups sugar
2   tablespoons white wine vinegar
2   tablespoons julienned peeled ginger
2   tablespoons julienned orange rind
1   cup fresh orange juice
6   cups fresh cranberries
2   small tart apples, peeled, finely chopped
1   cup toasted slivered almonds

Pour the boiling water over the raisins in a small bowl. Let stand for 15 minutes.

Bring the sugar and vinegar to a boil in a heavy saucepan over medium-low heat, stirring to dissolve the sugar. Increase the heat. Boil for 10 minutes or until the syrup is golden brown; remove from the heat. Stir in the ginger and orange rind. Add the orange juice. Bring to a boil, stirring constantly. Add the cranberries. Cook for 5 minutes or until the cranberries stop popping. Add the raisins, apples and almonds; mix well. Cool to room temperature. Chill, covered, for up to 2 days.

RED ONION AND APPLE CHUTNEY

Serves 10

A tasty and pretty addition to a pork roast or holiday ham.

2/3 cup warm water
1/4 cup cider vinegar
3   tablespoons honey
1   cup golden raisins
1/8 teaspoon dried mint (optional)
     Ground cloves to taste
4   cups thinly sliced red onion quarters
3   tablespoons vegetable oil
2   tablespoons unsalted butter
1   Granny Smith apple, chopped
     Salt and pepper to taste

Combine the water, vinegar, honey, raisins, mint and cloves in a small bowl; mix well. Let stand for several minutes.

Cook the onions in the oil and butter in a large covered skillet over medium-low heat for 15 minutes or until tender. Cook, uncovered, for 30 minutes longer or until very tender, stirring frequently. Add the raisin mixture and apple. Cook over medium heat until the liquid has evaporated and the apple is tender, stirring constantly. Season with salt and pepper. Store, covered, in the refrigerator. Serve at room temperature.

NEW PICKLES

Serves 30

A different and easy treat for the family and for gifts.

1   (46-ounce) jar kosher dill pickles
3   cups sugar
3/4 cup white vinegar
2   tablespoons pickling spice

Pour the juice from the pickles; cut each pickle into 3/4-inch pieces; return to the jar. Combine the sugar, vinegar and pickling spice in a medium saucepan. Bring to a boil, stirring to dissolve the sugar completely. Pour over the pickles. Cool slightly. Seal the jar. Chill for 24 hours or longer before serving.

CRÈME FRAÎCHE

Serves 8

Serve crème fraîche sweetened with desserts or use unsweetened in casseroles, gratins and cream soups.

1   cup whipping cream
3   tablespoons buttermilk

Combine the cream and buttermilk in a wide-mouthed jar; cover with plastic wrap. Let stand at room temperature for 24 to 36 hours or until thickened, stirring every 6 to 12 hours. Refrigerate, covered, for up to 3 weeks.

FRUIT SAUCE

Serves 8

Serve with assorted fresh fruit such as melon, pineapple, bananas, apples or grapes as a light dessert or healthy snack.

1 cup orange-pineapple yogurt
4 ounces cream cheese, softened
2 tablespoons brown sugar
1/4 cup coconut

Combine the yogurt, cream cheese and brown sugar in a bowl; mix until smooth. Stir in the coconut. Chill until serving time.

WHERE'S-THE-FAT CHOCOLATE SAUCE

Serves 8

Serve warm or cooled over ice cream or as a dipping sauce for fruit or cake cubes.

3/4 cup sugar
1/3 cup baking cocoa
4 teaspoons cornstarch
2/3 cup evaporated milk
1 teaspoon vanilla extract

Mix the sugar, cocoa and cornstarch in a saucepan. Stir in the evaporated milk gradually. Cook over medium heat until thickened and bubbly, stirring constantly. Cook for 2 minutes longer, stirring constantly; remove from the heat. Stir in the vanilla.

DAFFODIL LEMON SAUCE

Serves 10 to 12

Serve this light sauce with angel food cake, white cake or bread pudding.

1/2   cup sugar
4   teaspoons cornstarch
1/8   teaspoon salt
1   cup water
1/2   cup egg substitute
1   tablespoon margarine
3   (to 4) tablespoons fresh lemon juice
1/2   (to 1) teaspoon grated lemon rind (optional)

Mix the sugar, cornstarch and salt in a saucepan. Stir in the water. Cook until thickened and bubbly, stirring frequently. Stir a small amount of the hot mixture into egg substitute; stir the egg substitute into the hot mixture. Add the margarine, lemon juice and lemon rind; mix well.

IRISH CREAM FROSTING

Serves 16

Wonderful on carrot cake or spice cake.

1   cup unsalted butter, softened
2 1/4 cups confectioners' sugar
1/2   teaspoon salt
1/4   cup Irish Cream

Cream the butter in a mixer bowl until light and fluffy. Add the confectioners' sugar gradually. Add the salt and liqueur; beat until the frosting is light and fluffy.

FABULOUS FLAKY PIE CRUST

Serves 6 to 8

This really is the flakiest pie pastry; chilling the dough makes it easier to handle.

1   cup flour
1/2   teaspoon salt
7 1/3 tablespoons shortening
2   tablespoons ice water

Mix the flour and salt in a bowl. Cut in the shortening until crumbly. Sprinkle the water 1 tablespoon at a time over the mixture, tossing lightly with a fork until the mixture forms a dough. Shape into a ball; flatten slightly. Chill, wrapped in plastic wrap, for 1 hour.

Roll on a lightly floured surface or between 2 sheets of waxed paper. Fit into pie plate; prick with fork. Bake at 450 degrees for 10 to 12 minutes or until golden brown or use filling and baking directions in your recipe.

MEMBERSHIP LIST

JoAnn Norman Allen
Carolyn Mattison Allison
Jean Wormley Anderson
Rae Kellner Anderson
Tressa Ginestra Anderson
Cathie Mullins Arenson
Shirley Upchurch Ax
Donna Johnson Bader
Marsha VanDerZwalm Baer
Carolyn Kent Bailey
Helen Smith Bailey
Phyllis Marshall Bailey
Sally Dickinson Baker
Harriet Bergen Barnard
Helen Scherwin Barrett
Maureen McGuire Basile
Helen Wolfensperger Beattie
Kathleen Mills Beatty
Emily Bedford
Lon Gersten Behr
Nadine Bright Bell
Norma Powers Bender
Suzanne Jeffries Bennett
Nancy Morris Bieck
Cheryl Metallo Bischoff
Kathryn Bischoff
Linda Wantz Bittle
Lorrie Blackler
Julie Bliss
Isabelle Geithman Boehmen
Jean Thompson Bordorff
Debbie Buckler Boswell
Suzanne Harrold Boswell
Tammy Niedner Bowman
Joan Daane Bradley
Amy Bradley-Thomas
Karen Aedo Brooks
Amy Becker Brown
Lisa Olander Brown
Tina Buffington Brown
Betsy Burgoyne
Cindy Ball Burns
Susan Busenbark
Drusie Taylor Bushnell
Sandra Rae Busjahn
Nancy Lewis Butler

Elise Huckabee Cadigan-Koski
Kathy Gray Campbell
Elaine Sommer Carlson
Tamira Nilson Carlson
Karen Carruthers
Mary-Stuart Johnstone Carruthers
Mary Bartlett Caskey
Barbara Sullivan Cavataio
Annmarie Heidenfelder Clark
Mary Gardner Clarke
Caryl Wilsman Clauson
Wendy Clauson-Knuth
Erna Engelkes Colborn
Barbara Cole
Kerry Miller Cole
Trudi Leetz Confort
Diane Snodgrass Conklin
Marcia Kaney Cook
Mary Cook
Mary Loughry Cook
Dr. Margaret Cooney
Ninette Basile Cooney
Sharon Lyon Cooper
Sue Fink Cowan
Cheryl Morgan Obrecht Crahan
Jean Licary Crosby
Janet Geiger Currier
Debra Atkinson Cyborski
Donna Leacott Davidson
Carlian Dawson
Judy Dern
Elizabeth Quest Dickinson
Christyn Bell Divine
Eleaner Funkhouser Doar
Nancy Ghent Donohue
Kirby Johnson Doyle
Marilyn Waling Doyle
Barb Glauert D'Souza
Mary VandeZande Duffy
Gail Behnke Edwards
Georganne Hinchliff Eggers
Shirley Fivek Eighmy
Lucy Goetz Eklund
Marjorie Anderson Elliot
Sandra Jeane Howe Elliot
Audrey Rossate Engelbrecht

Barbara Witty Erickson
Ellen Baitinger Erkert
Joan Matthews Erkert
Ida Prezioso Ewald
Katherine Eastman Faith
Patricia Harness Farney
Mary Ann Pittman Fearer
Jody Piepenburg Fenelon
Pamela Gerhardt Ferguson
Amy Younglove Fish
Penny Hummel Fisher
Suzanne Yake Floody
Mary Glen Foster
Jodi Foster-Weber
Margaret More Fourie
Carol Janicki Fredrickson
Andrea Freed-Krehbiel
Holly Froning
Catherine Ward Funderburg
Sylvia Bruscato Gaffney
Barbara Feldman Gagliano
Barbara Ferrell Gaines
Barbara Bennett Galloway
Kay Lievens Galloway
Margaret Milani Galvan
Barbara Brockmeier Gambino
Deborah Russell Gardner
Nan McDonald Geddeis
Judy Lundeen Geissler
Katie Snyder Gifford
Karen Hentschel Gilbert
Kathy Keller Giovingo
Nancy Monday Glass
Patricia Meyers Gleichman
Sally Knukle Goddard
Jody Johnson Goff
Shelley Govig
Honore Burns Greenwald
Penny Gregory
Vicky Grondski
Geraldine Nosalik Gustafson
Gloria Mortellaro Gustafson
Kathy Ginestra Guzzardo
Christine Frieman Haeggquist
Anne Giliberti Hagney
Denis Allen Hall

Lea Blackburn Halsey
Missy DiSalvo Hand
Darlene Myers Hanna
Patricia Grossner Harker
Eileen Hyland Harner
Marjorie Chandler Harnois
Marcella Eason Harris
Mary Schindel Harris
LaDonna Hopper Hartman
Jane Wilhelmus Hawkins
Joanne Mera Heckinger
Diane Anderson Hedberg
Jean Carlson Hembrough
Mary Alice Eastman Hermanson
Barbara Hernmann
Nancy Logan Hill
Joan Otis Hinken
Lori Finnegan Hitzke
Kathryn Hobart
Sally Klingensmith Hoff
Jennifer Hohn
Judith Healey Holder
Shirley Sommer Holzwarth
Andrea Kupl Homann
Elizabeth Nash Homewood
Jean Beecher Horihan
Peggy Cullen Humpal
Sue Ralston Humphris
Susan Brostedt Huntting
Maura Kreuz Hurless
Martha Ashley Hutt
Sara Yang HuYoung
Nancy Guyer Hyzer
Jeanne Grahn Ilseman
Teresa O'Donnell Ingrassia
Jill Fritzlen Jackson
Jennifer Dillion Jacobs
Karen Liesman Jasper
Phoebe Johnson Jeffreys
Diann Jakubek Johnson
Georgeann Allen Johnson
Julie Holmberg Johnson
Kimberly Johnson
Michelle Tulley Johnson
Patricia Michaels Johnson
Barbara Kaiser

Donna Prindle Kamish
Carole Gersten Kaplan
Lynda Peterson Kennedy
Carla Shaff Kieckhefer
Lesley Bork Killoren
Molly Klazura
Sharon Klint
Jeanne Delong Knowland
Fran Castrogiovanni Knutson
Darlene Hayes Koerner
Vicky Nichols Kohlbacher
Janet Locknar Konicek
Pauline Koplos Kostantacos
Jean Wheeler Kramer
Linda Bermea Krause
Jennifer Hinken Krinickas
Lauren Kapper Kronenberg
Mary Thalacker Kuller
Betsy Merrill Kunkel
Barb Lehman Kurilla
Cynthia May Larson
Judy Anderson Larson
Barbara Tarabori LaSalle
Sharon Lyons Lassandro
Elizabeth Rhodes Lawton
Anita Ahlgren Layng
Ann Biggerstaff Leefers
Grace Hartman Leighton
Helen Leonard
Ellen Trevan Letourneau
Betty Thorpe Lillie
Jeannette Anderson Lindman
Terri Green Lindmark
Kathryn Wiley Link
Oma Olive Littleton
Galey Shappert Lucas
Katherine Pearce Luchetti
Beth Stoner Lukas
Nancy Hovet Lundstrom
Jane Lyons
Susan Paustian Manas
Jan Marion
Jane Smith Marlowe
Marianne Davis Marshall
Kathyrn Rundquist Mattison
Nancy Shappert Mattison

Elaine Brown Mayfield
Beverlie Briggs Maynard
Sanchia Bruer Mazza
Joyce Myers Mazzola
Carroll Adams McCarthy
Betsy McCoy
Elizabeth Brearly McDonald
Mary (Betsy) McIntosh
Kathy McNeely-Johnson
Wilma Schrag McNess
Hallie McPhee-Johnstone
Sheila McPherson
Diane Parkhurst Meltmar
Sindy Stutz Micho Mills
Lynn Miani Moczynski
Susan Fransen Moore
Ann Bluth More
Kathleen Lerche Morman
Doris Clausius Mosser
Phyllis Mark Mott
Molly Possehl Moyna
Barbara Carlson Mueller
Maureen Mooney Murphy
Janet Conley Murray
Julie Barber Murray
Jane Nappi-Lindstrand
Jo Needham Nash
Lois Sandy Nelson
Sharon Lange Nelson
Constance Stanley Nethercut
Carole Sanders Newcomer
Ruth Whitehead Nicholas
Rachel Brauchle Nichols
Ruth Scudder Nihan
Sandra Jacobson Nilsson
Julie Johannes Nimtz
Lucy Berger Nora
Jody Stafford Nordlof
Beverly Barber North
Peggy Clark Northrop
Gwen Jacobs Novak
Shawn Gorman Novak
Eileen O'Hagen-Tillis
Denise Countryman Oliver
Courtney Read Olson
Nancy Nichols Olson

Jane Heil Ott
Claudia Render Owens
Melissa Pappas
Connie Hinton Paris
JoMarie Moerschel Paul
Lisbeth Lindquist Pearson
Patty Pember
Claire Bandelin Perkins
Judith Reddish Peterson
Carlyn Bruce Peterson
Cathryn Dalvey Peterson
Diane Stamm Peterson
Trudy Bacak Philipp
Sharon Bressler Pierce
Elizabeth Reddy Pierson
Heidi Baker Pitman
Norma Futerman Polcek
Martha Brown Porter
Mary Bodaken Powell
Beverly Hughes Preiss
Karen Schulstrom Preiss
Diane Lietz Provi
Rebecca Boydens Pshirrer
Mary Brady Raines
Lori Olson Rasmann
Cynthia Reed
Jean Whitehead Reese
Teri Wright Reynolds
Trudy Gassmann Reynolds
Virginia Weleck Rickin
Roberta Ameling Ricklefs
Cheryl Melman Rinker
Pat Spraker Ritz
Chris Dorsey Roarty
Betty Hausz Roska
Dawn McCook Rudie
Sherri Rudy
Mary Littrell Rudzinski
Shirley Johnson Rundquist
Nancy Kraffert Russo
Marjorie Tullock Ryan

Patricia Davis Sanderson
Ann Morris Sarros
Gail Bauer Schauer
Carolyn Bence Schmidt
Joan Slausen Schmidt
Nancy Hobson Schroeder
Deanne Mikelson Schwanke
Marilyn Bygrave Schweisberger
JoAnn Cox Shaheen
Nancy Nott Shannon
Norma Bailey Shelden
Judy Hoover Sheley
Patricia Cryer Shepherd
Karen Reinhold Shifo
Margo Shifo
Peggy Cavitt Showers
Nancy Schmeling Shugart
Martha McNulty Shula
Suzanne Kauzlarich Sloan
Barbara Bygrave Smith
Betty Burrowa Smith
Martha Craft Smith
Tricia Cratty Smith
Lori Smith-Kosch
Paticia Murphy Sneed
Julie Smith Snively
Eleanor Anderson Snyder
Lynn Kania Splinter
Christie Peterson Stark
Vinest Jackson Steele
Ann Berg Stegall
Cassandra Steurer
Jennifer Stiles
Helen Dasenbrook Street
Suzette Fivaz Symes
Carol Giovingo Taphorn
Susan Nelson Taylor
Melissa Mehall Teske
Jane Depew Thappa
Catherine Wahlstrom Thiede
Margaret Powell Thienemann

Becky Aplington Thorsen
Karyl Yost Thorsen
Lisa Hartman Tomasino
Sandra Dolezal Tower
Betsie Kramp Trejo
Cynthia Johnson Troia
Gayle Noble Truitt
Francine Williams Tuite
Susan Milligan Turner
Carol Sargent Valaitis
Lynne Denham Vass
Barbara Giorgi Vella
Nancy Morgan Voss
Susan Powell Waldrip
Patricia Collier Waters
Leticia Hunel Webb
Julie Humpal Weber
Kathleen Beynon Weis
Susan Heege Weiss
Dimmis Lathrop Weller
Suzanne Shellenberger Welsh
Jaime Welte
Laurie Fuller Wharton
Mary Elizabeth Nobles Wheeler
Gail Hooks White
Beverly Williams Whitehead
Harriet Burpee Whitehead
Kathleen Szczepankowski Whiteley
Catherine Carr Wieder
Lois Blue Williams
Grace Radde Wilson
Maureen Healy Wirth
Sarah Beekman Wolf
Joann Worden
Jeanine Carlson Wortmann
Debbi Provi Wright
Polly Nyman Wright
Elizabeth Yock
Susan James York

COMMUNITY CONTRIBUTORS

Ruth Aedo
Jackie Allen
Nancy Arnold
Dorris Atkinson
Genevieve Bacak
Lisa Baker
Martha Barclay
Kris Barr
Linda Bartels
Diane Basile
Lynn Baylor-Zies
Britt Becker
Leanna Bell
Ruth Bender
Gina Biggins
Naomi Bloom
Mary Joan Brooks
Dorothy Brown
Wendy Brown
Colleen Buirle
Karen Burkholder
Geri Carlson
Sue Carlson
Chris Chapman
Lois Clauson
Karen Coobs
Hilder Dallman
Michelle Daniels
Nancy Morgan Davis
Lora Deane
Joy Dennison
Doris Dillon
Audrey Dittmar
Helen Dorr
Donna Drye
Rusty Dufoe
Shirley Eisfeller
Floyce Farmer
Linda Fenelon
Pat Floody
Norma Ford
JoEva Freeman
Kathy Gasparini
Diane Green

Lorelei Grossner
Sheila Hahn
JoHanna Harden
Pattie Harris
Margaret Ann Heckinger
Juliana Hejna
Martha Herrick
Annette Hidde
Kathy Hobbs
Carol Holton
Jan Hood
Diane Horne
Sally Iannucci
Peg Jeffrey
Julie Johnson
Kathy Johnson
Holly Johnstone
Nan Kammann
Jane Kasper
Kathlene Kelleher
Janet Klaas
Barb Kline
Betty Klingensmith
Carol Kloppmann
Verna Konicek
Isabel Krisor
Shari Lamers
Nancy Lamprecht
Elisabeth Lange
Renee Lange-Rinn
David Larson
Yvette Lefort
Holly Lembkey
Olga Letourneau
Susan Nelson Letourneau
Lisa Lindman
Lois Lockner
Stacy Lockner
Amy Loescher
Nancy May
Mary Mazzetti
Kathleen McCormick
Gladys McKinney
Barbara McNamara

June Mera
Alice Meyers
Linda Meyers
Rudy Miller
Ann Millings
Brenda Moore
Judy Moyna
Elaine Mueller
Mary Lynn Mullins
Colleen Murphy
Helen Murray
Leonard Musselman
Leslie Nautiyal
Elinor Nelson
Leah Nelson
Sylvia Nevtipil
Penny Niesen
Jeraldine Noll
Nancy Nora
Patricia Nora
Mary Alice Odling
Dorothy Olander
Amy Olson
Betty Onderdonk
Nancy Otterstrom
Janel Palmer
Beth L. Parentice
Helene Peach
Valerie Pederson
Anna Marie Peterson
Deb Peterson
Julie Phelps
Dorothy Philipp
Prof. & Mrs. Van K.
    Phillip
Cathy Phillips
Cynthia Possehl
Kathy Pozzi
Chad Preiss
Terri Price
Diane Provi
Jane Purin
Paula Jo Pyka
Irmgard Redweik

Clifford Reed
Kathleen Reed
Mrs. Lloyd Ringle
Carole Ringlespaugh
Karen Roberts
Atliva Rodefer
Colleen Runkle
Beth Rush
Stephanie Sandberg
Linda Schreiner
Dorothy Schuette
Connie Schultz
Donna Schultz
Clara Seibert
Sue Seidel
Gly Shaw
Martha Shearer
Alice Smoot
Helen Sorenson
Dale Sperud
Carol Stamm
Coline Sutherland
Diana Tarabori
Larry Taylor
Peg Teevan
Jaime Thayer
Emma Thompson
Nancy Thompson
Miriam Thor
JoEllen Vause
Lillian Veselik
Florence Warren
Betty Waterfield
Kathy Waterman
Jeanne Weberling
Sue Weese
Alice Weiss
Lorraine White
Robert A. White
Rose White
Elizabeth Winkler
Millie Wright
Martha Zimmerman

SUBSTITUTIONS

	INSTEAD OF	USE
BAKING	1 teaspoon baking powder	1/4 teaspoon soda plus 1/2 teaspoon cream of tartar
	1 tablespoon cornstarch (for thickening)	2 tablespoons flour or 1 tablespoon tapioca
	1 cup sifted all-purpose flour	1 cup plus 2 tablespoons sifted cake flour
	1 cup sifted cake flour	1 cup minus 2 tablespoons sifted all-purpose flour
	1 cup dry bread crumbs	3/4 cup cracker crumbs
DAIRY	1 cup buttermilk	1 cup sour milk or 1 cup yogurt
	1 cup heavy cream	3/4 cup skim milk plus 1/3 cup butter
	1 cup light cream	7/8 cup skim milk plus 3 tablespoons butter
	1 cup sour cream	7/8 cup sour milk plus 3 tablespoons butter
	1 cup sour milk	1 cup milk plus 1 tablespoon vinegar or lemon juice or 1 cup buttermilk
SEASONING	1 teaspoon allspice	1/2 teaspoon cinnamon plus 1/8 teaspoon cloves
	1 cup catsup	1 cup tomato sauce plus 1/2 cup sugar plus 2 tablespoons vinegar
	1 clove of garlic	1/8 teaspoon garlic powder or 1/8 teaspoon instant minced garlic or 3/4 teaspoon garlic salt or 5 drops of liquid garlic
	1 teaspoon Italian spice	1/4 teaspoon each oregano, basil, thyme, rosemary plus dash of cayenne
	1 teaspoon lemon juice	1/2 teaspoon vinegar
	1 tablespoon mustard	1 teaspoon dry mustard
	1 medium onion	1 tablespoon dried minced onion or 1 teaspoon onion powder
SWEET	1 1-ounce square chocolate	1/4 cup cocoa plus 1 teaspoon shortening
	1 2/3 ounces semisweet chocolate	1 ounce unsweetened chocolate plus 4 teaspoons granulated sugar
	1 cup honey	1 to 1 1/4 cups sugar plus 1/4 cup liquid or 1 cup corn syrup or molasses
	1 cup granulated sugar	1 cup packed brown sugar or 1 cup corn syrup, molasses or honey minus 1/4 cup liquid

EQUIVALENTS

	WHEN THE RECIPE CALLS FOR	USE
BAKING	½ cup butter	4 ounces
	2 cups butter	1 pound
	4 cups all-purpose flour	1 pound
	4½ to 5 cups sifted cake flour	1 pound
	1 square chocolate	1 ounce
	1 cup semisweet chocolate chips	6 ounces
	4 cups marshmallows	1 pound
	2¼ cups packed brown sugar	1 pound
	4 cups confectioners' sugar	1 pound
	2 cups granulated sugar	1 pound
CEREAL – BREAD	1 cup fine dry bread crumbs	4 to 5 slices
	1 cup soft bread crumbs	2 slices
	1 cup small bread cubes	2 slices
	1 cup fine cracker crumbs	28 saltines
	1 cup fine graham cracker crumbs	15 crackers
	1 cup vanilla wafer crumbs	22 wafers
	1 cup crushed cornflakes	3 cups uncrushed
	4 cups cooked macaroni	8 ounces uncooked
	3½ cups cooked rice	1 cup uncooked
DAIRY	1 cup shredded cheese	4 ounces
	1 cup cottage cheese	8 ounces
	1 cup sour cream	8 ounces
	1 cup whipped cream	½ cup heavy cream
	⅔ cup evaporated milk	1 small can
	1⅔ cups evaporated milk	1 13-ounce can
FRUIT	4 cups sliced or chopped apples	4 medium
	1 cup mashed bananas	3 medium
	2 cups pitted cherries	4 cups unpitted
	2½ cups shredded coconut	8 ounces
	4 cups cranberries	1 pound
	1 cup pitted dates	1 8-ounce package
	1 cup candied fruit	1 8-ounce package
	3 to 4 tablespoons lemon juice plus 1 tablespoon grated lemon rind	1 lemon
	⅓ cup orange juice plus 2 teaspoons grated orange rind	1 orange
	4 cups sliced peaches	8 medium
	2 cups pitted prunes	1 12-ounce package
	3 cups raisins	1 15-ounce package

EQUIVALENTS

	WHEN THE RECIPE CALLS FOR	USE
MEATS	4 cups chopped cooked chicken 3 cups chopped cooked meat 2 cups cooked ground meat	1 5-pound chicken 1 pound, cooked 1 pound, cooked
NUTS	1 cup chopped nuts	4 ounces shelled 1 pound unshelled
VEGETABLES	2 cups cooked green beans 2½ cups lima beans or red beans 4 cups shredded cabbage 1 cup grated carrot 8 ounces fresh mushrooms 1 cup chopped onion 4 cups sliced or chopped potatoes 2 cups canned tomatoes	½ pound fresh or 1 16-ounce can 1 cup dried, cooked 1 pound 1 large 1 4-ounce can 1 large 4 medium 1 16-ounce can

MEASUREMENT EQUIVALENTS

1 tablespoon = 3 teaspoons	4 quarts = 1 gallon
2 tablespoons = 1 ounce	1 6½ to 8-ounce can = 1 cup
4 tablespoons = ¼ cup	1 10½ to 12-ounce can = 1¼ cups
5⅓ tablespoons = ⅓ cup	1 14 to 16-ounce can = 1¾ cups
8 tablespoons = ½ cup	1 16 to 17-ounce can = 2 cups
12 tablespoons = ¾ cup	1 18 to 20-ounce can = 2½ cups
16 tablespoons = 1 cup	1 29-ounce can = 3½ cups
1 cup = 8 ounces or ½ pint	1 46 to 51-ounce can = 5¾ cups
4 cups = 1 quart	1 6½ to 7½-pound can or Number 10 = 12 to 13 cups

METRIC EQUIVALENTS

Liquid	Dry
1 teaspoon = 5 milliliters	1 quart = 1 liter
1 tablespoon = 15 milliliters	1 ounce = 30 grams
1 fluid ounce = 30 milliliters	1 pound = 450 grams
1 cup = 250 milliliters	2.2 pounds = 1 kilogram
1 pint = 500 milliliters	

NOTE: The metric measures are approximate benchmarks for purposes of home food preparation.

HERBS

Use fresh whole herbs when possible. When fresh herbs are not available, use whole dried herbs that can be crushed just while adding. Store herbs in airtight containers away from the heat of the stove. Fresh herbs may be layered between paper towels and dried in the microwave on HIGH for 2 minutes or until dry.

Basil . . . . Can be chopped and added to cold poultry salads. If the recipe calls for tomatoes or tomato sauce, add a touch of basil to bring out a rich flavor.

Bay leaf . . . . The basis of many French seasonings. It is added to soups, stews, marinades and stuffings.

Bouquet garni . . . . . A bundle of parsley, thyme and bay leaves tied together and added to stews, soups or sauces. Other herbs and spices may be added to the basic herbs.

Chervil . . . . One of the traditional fines herbes used in French cooking. (The others are tarragon, parsley and chives.) It is good in omelets and soups.

Chives . . . . Available fresh, dried or frozen, it can be substituted for raw onion or shallot in nearly any recipe.

Garlic . . . . One of the oldest herbs in the world, it must be carefully handled. For best results, press or crush the garlic clove.

Marjoram . . . . An aromatic herb of the mint family, it is good in soups, sauces, stuffings and stews.

Mint . . . . Use fresh, dried or ground with vegetables, desserts, fruits, jelly, lamb or tea. Fresh sprigs of mint make attractive aromatic garnishes.

Oregano . . . . A staple, savory herb in Italian, Spanish, Greek and Mexican cuisines. It is very good in dishes with a tomato foundation, especially in combination with basil.

Parsley . . . . Use this mild herb as fresh sprigs or dried flakes to flavor or garnish almost any dish.

Rosemary . . . . This pungent herb is especially good in poultry and fish dishes and in such accompaniments as stuffings.

Saffron . . . . Use this deep orange herb, made from the dried stamens of a crocus, sparingly in poultry, seafood and rice dishes.

Sage . . . . This herb is a perennial favorite used with all kinds of poultry and stuffing dishes.

Tarragon . . . . One of the fines herbes. Goes well with all poultry dishes, whether hot or cold.

Thyme . . . . Usually used in combination with bay leaf in soups, stews and sauces.

SPICES

Spices should be stored in airtight containers away from the heat of the stove or in the refrigerator. Add ground spices toward the end of the cooking time to retain maximum flavor. Whole spices may be added at the beginning but should have a small amount of additional spices added near the end of cooking time also.

Allspice	Pungent aromatic spice, whole or in powdered form. It is excellent in marinades, particularly in game marinade, or in curries.
Caraway seeds	Use the whole seeds in breads, especially rye, and with cheese, sauerkraut and cabbage dishes.
Celery seeds	Use whole or ground in salad dressings, sauces or pickles or in meat, cheese, egg and fish dishes.
Chili powder	Made from dried red chili peppers, this spice ranges from mild to fiery depending on the type of chili pepper used. Used especially in Mexican cooking, it is a delicious addition to eggs, dips and sauces.
Cinnamon	Ground from the bark of the cinnamon tree, it is delicious in desserts as well as in savory dishes.
Coriander	Seeds used whole or ground, this slightly lemony spice adds an unusual flavor to soups, stews, chili dishes, curries and desserts.
Curry powder	A blend of several spices, this gives Indian cooking its characteristic flavor.
Cumin	A staple spice in Mexican cooking. Use in meat, rice, cheese, egg and fish dishes.
Ginger	The whole root used fresh, dried or ground is a sweet, pungent addition to desserts or oriental-style dishes.
Mustard (dry)	Ground mustard seeds bring a sharp bite to sauces or may be sprinkled sparingly over poultry or other foods.
Nutmeg	Use the whole spice or a bit of freshly ground for flavor in beverages, breads and desserts. A sprinkle on top is both a flavor enhancer and an attractive garnish.
Pepper	Black and white pepper from the pepperberry or peppercorn, whether whole, ground or cracked, is the most commonly used spice in or on any food.
Poppy seeds	Use these tiny, nut-flavored seeds in salad dressings, breads and cakes or as a flavorful garnish for cheese, rolls or noodle dishes.
Turmeric	Ground from a root related to ginger, this is an essential in curry powder. Also used in pickles and relishes and in cheese and egg dishes.

INDEX

For order information contact:

Junior League of Rockford, Inc.
4118 Pinecrest Road
Rockford, Illinois 61107
1-800-455-8225